# WITH LOVE SIR

Prof (Dr) Sanjay Mohan Johri

First Published in October 2022

**ISBN: 978-93-5704-118-8**

**BLUEROSE PUBLISHERS**

www.BlueRoseONE.com

info@bluerosepublishers.com

+91 8882 898 898

**Cover Design:**

Shirish Sharma & Mohit Sharma

**Image:**

Trilochan S Kalra

**Typographic Design:**

Namrata Saini

**Distributed by:** BlueRose, Amazon, Flipkart

# Contents

## Retracing the journey, step by step!

*"Mentoring is a brain to pick, an ear to listen, and a push in the right direction."* - John Crosby

Mentoring is a concept that has expanded in definition in recent years to include non-traditional relationships beyond face-to-face mentoring. Long considered as an effective tool for developing relationships and transferring knowledge from a more experienced individual to a less experienced individual, mentoring helps learners acclimate to a new academic atmosphere as they move from secondary education to higher education in universities, particularly in India. It's a relationship which takes time to understand each other & students try to rely on the expertise and experience of their mentors (teachers) to help them graduate and develop as professionals for their roadmap they have in mind.

Mentoring students doesn't mean acting like their parents — or their best friends, says Benjamin Shank, (CEO of American Higher Education Alliance (AHEA)), adding: "*Mentoring should be considered a critical element to student success.*"

Mentoring is a valuable strategy to provide students with the emotional and instrumental support students need to achieve the goal of a college degree. By providing information, guidance, and encouragement, mentors play an important role in nurturing students.

Mentoring programmes in the 21st century is no longer thought of as just the traditional pairings such as teacher and student, but now non-traditional relationships can be formed either electronically, with groups or peers, or a combination of several types. The programmes now usually extend beyond face-to-face mentoring and are frequently supported by technology. While one-on-one mentoring is used in most programs, and is the model most people prefer, technology is creating opportunities for more individuals to be mentored and to be mentored internationally by a global mentor through expanding geographic boundaries.

At Amity University, the unique Mentor-Mentee Concept ensures constant interaction between the faculty and the students. A faculty member is assigned to a group of 5-6 students to counsel them on their academic and personal concerns. Their experience helps students gain the confidence and skills they need to face challenges both in their academic pursuits and their progression into the professional world. We want students to never feel away from home and to share their problems, both personal & emotional.

Having been with Amity University for over 13 years now, I not only tried to work upon the Mentoring system with my faculty colleagues but also ventured into picking up a good number of Mentees & evolving a mechanism to help them identify their professional goals and guide them throughout their academics and as they move into higher education. Besides being a field journalist with India's premier news agency, the Press Trust of India, for over 20 years and then into media academics as a visiting faculty with the University of Lucknow, Bhartiya Vidya Bhavan's Lal Bahadur Shastri Institute of Communication Studies (LBS), Jaipuria Institute of Management, and then to Amity University, I am happy I could maintain a bond with all my Mentees at personal and professional level & the journey continues.

It was just a coincidence that one of my Mentees, Ms. Punjya Singh, who is now in Melbourne, visited India when the pandemic struck, and had to stay back for over one year. We discussed the idea of this book and sought feedback from

Mentees both in India and abroad. They responded positively and were quite excited about this. They promised to look back at their journey and write testimonials. Since the number was quite large, I decided to pick those who responded in a given time frame, and 41 of them have beautifully written testimonials about their journey in Mentoring.

Punyja is credited for her help in compiling and editing the testimonials and contributing her own experiences. Avnish Srivastava, an ex-Jaipurian and now Assistant Editor, Times of India, my colleagues Mohit Sharma, Shirish Sharma, and Trilochan S. Kalra, all came together and helped in the production of this book “With Love Sir” by sharing their expertise.

There could have been no better person than Prof (Dr) S.Z.H. Zaidi, a veteran in the field of Psychology & Director, Amity School of Behavioural Sciences, to write the **Prologue** and our very own Pro Vice Chancellor, Prof (Dr) Sunil Dhaneshwar, for the **Epilogue**. My two senior colleagues with whom I have worked for many years, Mr. Ratan Mani Lal, and Prof. Chander Mahadev, have shared their experiences on Mentoring & my association with them.

At Amity University, students' support and progression is the main objective of the Mentor-Mentee program to inspire, recognize their potential, strengthen their varied capabilities & to build an interpersonal relationship to pursue their destined dreams.

I am sure this book will be worth reading for the current batches as well as for the students entering higher education to understand the importance of mentoring and shape their future.

**Prof. (Dr) Sanjay M Johri**

# Prologue

## Mentor-mentee share long-term ties beyond college learning

Mentorship is a process in which an expert having long professional experience and exposure to different situations helps develop an individual, i.e., his 'Mentee' in the multifield dimensions including selection, induction, and progression into a specific career suitable for him/her. The mentor often has two primary functions for his mentee such as career related function, where he provides intensive support, skill, and knowhow as coach to establish his mentee in the career suitable and relevant to him. And also, as an advisor or counsellor to empower his mentee, who may take the right decision independently and at the right time and to create a position in a competitive world and global society. In Indian system of philosophy, mentoring is not a new concept or a support system. Mentoring or its practice finds its roots in Indian mythology where lord Krishna mentors Arjun during the Kurukshetra war in the Indian epic "Mahabharata". In ancient Indian history, we also find various great mentors like Chanakya, who mentored Chandragupta Maurya to not only conquer and consolidate the large empire but also coach him to be a great philosopher and ruler.

In the recent past, the Mentor-Mentee system has been introduced in the academic system in a more formal way, but the sole of the mentor-mentee philosophy is a much more dynamic, need-based, and long-term relationship beyond the classroom and the boundary walls of colleges and universities.

The relationship of mentor-mentee is built upon well-defined factors such as trust and respect, an open and honest communication, flexibility, and understanding of other perspectives. Dr. J.S. Neki, an eminent psychiatrist, has defined the concept of "Guru-Chela relationship" in his classical publication in which he identified the characteristics of a counsellor or therapist as "Guru" and their client as "Chela", who not only submit and open before his Guru but also, expects his guru to shape his life and career by carving and cutting, polishing and rubbing as and when required.

An ideal mentor-mentee process should benefit mentees in the following broad ways-

### 1. Increased Self-Confidence

Self-confidence can be defined in different ways, but the operational definition of self-confidence can be "faith in one-self", meaning thereby the mentee should start trusting his own abilities and effectiveness in handling difficult situations. The mentor should make attempts to develop self-confidence in his mentee, which should be based on a demonstratable realistic approach and not only wishful thinking.

### 2. Increased Self-awareness

Self-actualisation or awareness about his own assets and liabilities is one of the very basic features or requirements for obtaining sustainable well-being. A mentor should work for making his mentee aware of his realistic profile and also help him to minimise the gaps.

### 3. Development of Communication Skills

Communication skill are the basis of effective connectivity and expression of emotions and thought processes. Communication is not only the channel for the transfer of ideas and thoughts but also a healthy way of expressing feelings which might go a long way in causing and healing t wounds and cementing relationships. From time immemorial there has not been any substitute for effective communication skills. The mentor should work on improving and making the communication skills to help to accommodate and flourish in all situations, particularly in communication skills which is required for the career he is opting for.

**4. Exposure to new and different perspectives**

One of the reasons for fast development in all spheres is the increasing curiosity to think differently and explore new perspectives. And perhaps that is why the length of the generation gap has reduced from two to three decades to a few months. Every professional is trying new concepts experimenting with established theories to retest their relevance in global scenarios. A mentor should hold the hand of his mentee to think out of the box and try with perspectives without compromising with the professional ethics.

**5. Networking and Periodical Updating**

The present era is the era of inter-disciplinary and constant support in the form of give and take intellectual properties which also requires good networking with the person who matter either in career or in dealing with the issues of everyday life-situations. Mentor should support his mentee to develop effective connectivity based on win-win situation that leads to global well-being so that his mentee may learn from the experiences of others.

As referred above, some of the important elements of mentor-mentee system are that the process and the relationship so developed are not only limited to classrooms and might go beyond the teaching environment. And also, it encourages long term relations starting from hand holding to taking the mentee till the door of success. But above process has to be handled within professional boundaries, considering ethical norms and the ability to discriminate between professional relations and transference, where in, the shift of emotions is possible, which is not only intense but inappropriate.

I am sure the book by Prof. Sanjay Mohan Johri, Professor and Director, Amity School of Communication, Amity University Lucknow Campus will be a landmark publication in the concept and process of Mentor-Mentee activities in teaching setup and beyond.

**Prof S Z H Zaidi**

**Director AIBAS Amity University (Lucknow Campus)**

(Dr. Zafar Zaidi, recipient of a National Award for his contributions to the Disability and Mental Health Sector, has 43 years of professional experience in India & Scotland.)

# Mentoring

## Like Krishna to Arjun, a mentor helps mentee tread the right path

There can be no better explanation of true Mentor-Mentee relationships than that of *Dronacharya* & *Arjun* or *Shri Krishna* and *Arjun* in the epic 'Mahabharat' or *Vashishtha* & *Ram* in Ramayana. Every student has a teacher or guru like Arjun had Dronacharya, but the teacher also tutors other students, like what *Dronacharya* did for the *Kauravas* and the *Pandava.*

The concept of mentoring is as old as the human race; every student has a teacher or guru too, and we can see many instances in our mythology where a mentor helps his/ her mentee realize and attain their full potential.

Of late, we have been focusing on the role of mentor-mentee relationship in the current higher education system, especially in Indian Universities as the mentor's duty has always been to protect the mentee from any imminent danger by giving proper advice and nurturing his/her growth personally & professionally. It is even more important for a mentee to find a mentor who can guide and lead you towards success amidst the present complexities of life and career.

Guru, Gurukul and Guru Purnima are concepts from ancient Indian Vedic tradition and possibly other cultures, which refer to a monastic style of learning. Mentoring is required in almost all walks of life and has been prevalent in our society.

A student in the present competitive world faces numerous situations and complexities that make it hard for him/ her to achieve the dreams what he/she aspires. Someone must explain and guide, and this is where Mentoring of students is even more important today, to address the near-unlimited, unbounded, and unprecedented access to all types of information. A true relationship between a mentor & mentee thus helps in guiding as to how one should progress systematically.

I remember with the recent havoc wreaked by the Covid-19 pandemic since March 2020 a nationwide lockdown forced educational institutions to close, and students went into Online classes. Prolonged lockdown and the continuance of Online classes posed mental stress among students. The second wave hit hard, and a large number of students got affected by the dreaded virus, with many facing mental issues. In many homes financial crisis and loss of job impacted children and youth.

There was sudden pressure on faculty to go in for regular mentoring sessions with students and counsel them to cope up with this unprecedented situation and maintain balance, as authorities were of the firm opinion that mentorship has an even greater importance. Glued to laptop screens throughout the day, the performance of all students was affected.

I have always believed mentoring is not something you do in a particular situation, but the kind of pressures we face in this competitive market, students remain confused as they enter into higher education, and look to their teachers for career-oriented and goal-oriented learning. A mentor shares information about their personal or others' life journey towards their career path with their mentee. They provide guidance, motivation, emotional support, and can even serve as role models and in general this must be focus of every mentor towards a mentee.

A mentor may help with exploring careers, setting goals, developing contacts, and identifying resources. Tutoring, guardianship, and mentoring activities have the same objectives. Parents, teachers, senior students, colleagues, friends, or any member of society with a suitable background can serve as a mentor to help with learning and motivation.

Mentoring is, however, not everyone's cup of tea because there can be no short cuts to the entire process you undertake. You need to watch your mentee, talk, and understand the confusion. You should have prolonged sessions and interactions to see the potential and talent and make him/her convinced of what he/she can do.

These activities were inseparable in the ancient Indian *Gurukul* education system, where a student simply used to surrender himself to the grace of his guru, staying away from society in a monastic setting with the guru's family.

In higher education, teachers are named as tutor-guardians and senior students are appointed as mentors or peer-mentors, with new or junior students as their mentees. It is quite possible for a mentor-mentee relationship to last for many years where appropriate, although as part of a formal system, it must be subject to regular review, evaluation, and monitoring.

An effective mentor with advanced knowledge or proven accomplishment in some field can offer leadership and guidance to help grow the professional capability of learners and colleagues they support.

An effective mentor having a sound domain or pedagogical knowledge and skill base for their role can establish respectful and effective mentoring relationships. Mentoring can offer multiple perspectives that can make education very relevant to the immediate challenges of our surroundings.

Research indicates that with good teacher mentoring programs, the quality of teaching and learning offered by inductee teachers is demonstrably more effective, and they may experience less stress, anxiety, and risk of attrition.

Interestingly, National Education Policy 2020, has taken up mentoring a National Mission. Govt. of India through Ministry of Education, University Grants Commission and AICTE are organizing various activities like orientation training programmes/mentoring workshops for mentors/faculty to make mentoring more relevant.

NEP-2020 focuses educational institutes and teachers to give more stress towards mentoring of students, so that students feel safe, protected, motivated, and free to share their thoughts with their teachers in the spirit of open-minded enquiry.

I came across with a good number of students and young minds during my 40 odd years journey into the media industry and media academics and first worked upon as to how a talent should be spotted and watch for his/her skills and aspirations. They were at a tender age, had just passed out of secondary education and found a completely new atmosphere when they entered the portals of university. Not all, but the majority of them had a lot of confusion, inhibitions and were hesitant to open. Perhaps someone had to hear them out and give them a sense of confidence. Few were single parent child, had seen separation or even domestic violence in the family, or were under the pressure of an education loan and wanted to prove and become a proud child for the family.

In majority of the cases, they had neither parent to share nor peers to discuss about the problems they faced but looked around one who can understand and guide them.

This is the time where a mentor plays a very important role in understanding and guiding a student to the right path, he/she deserves. If not in thousands but for sure in hundreds, I had the privilege to pick 'my mentees' both boys and girls and build a relationship, not for a year but in fact life-long and see his/her growth till he/she achieves what he/she aspired to.

I have tried through this book wherein I will not be sharing my own experiences as to how I helped 'My Mentees' to grow as professional but even 'Mentees' will write about their journey.

As a matter of fact, most of the available literature on mentoring focuses merely on its style, impact, and significance. Whereas the fundamentals of my book are based on the compilation of the existing examples which further directs the readers into pragmatic and relativistic thinking.

The most unique aspect of this book is that it is for both mentees and aspiring mentors. This book doesn't impose or restrict the readers thoughts, but rather leads them to both inductive and deductive reasoning based on the given situations to deal with, to further draw a practical conclusion.

**Prof (Dr) Sanjay M Johri**

# Mentors' Perspective

## A Journey from Handholding to A Bond That Lasts Forever

How do you define a 'Mentor'? A trusted Counsellor or a Guide or someone who gives a younger person help & advice over a period to see the Mentee succeed in life.

As you enter the portals of higher education institutions after your secondary education, you are into an unfamiliar environment and as you grow into an adult you find yourself in a new situation you have not confronted before. Yes, you have lot of aspirations, dreams in life to be a successful person but you need someone to understand and help you steer in the right direction.

A strong Mentor- Mentee program should be structured to build a mentor-mentee relationship where two minds require commitment to each other & their time. Amity university does have such a program, and in many campuses across India & abroad it has shown remarkable success. Its success solely depends on how a professor develops himself as a leader and helps develop his mentees into a professional and future leader in their respective fields.

Mentor- Mentee need to form a personal connection, understand each other's principles and values, strengths, and weaknesses, what drives them, and what they wish to achieve out of this relationship. You need to share values like integrity, mutual respect, openness, trust, and active listening as the basis for all the conversations you are likely to have.

Personally, I have followed most of these principles and today I can vouch for not only building lifetime relationships with my mentees, but I also love to see them achieving milestones in their career. The Girls certainly outnumbered boys perhaps they are more focused and serious towards their goal and at least this is clear with the testimonials shared in this book.

The relationship between a mentor and a mentee is unique as Mentors play a crucial role in the personal and professional growth of a mentee. They serve as guides for those who need someone to steer them to success. "However, mentoring is a two-way street in which the mentor and mentee play unique roles." This necessitates both taking responsibility and actively participating. "The mentorship will bloom into a useful connection if both participants are a symbiotic match."

It is an established fact that "As a mentor, you will provide guidance and support to your protege as they navigate complex and challenging situations in their career."

Refer "11 Best Practices for University Mentoring Programs - *Chronus*" whether it is preparing students to pursue the career of their dreams or connecting alumni with students or peers to network within their chosen field, university mentoring programmes are vital to the academic ecosystem.

Mentoring relationship for me is a nurturing process where I tried to inspire, train, counsel, and befriend a student as a mentee from the beginning. For me, it is over 40 years now both as a media professional and academician and I am glad my mentees from Lucknow University to Jaipuria Institute of Management and now at Amity University are in the industry occupying various positions in India & abroad and our lifetime relationship continues even today. I had young colleagues during my 20 long years with the Press Trust of India and I am happy I could guide them to see them reaching top position in the media industry.

For me, Mentorship has never been a "do it on the side" or "when I get time" job. It is really demanding work that requires dedication and commitment, much like any other part of our job. I evolved a mechanism to ensure that I stay connected with my mentees and with the technology evolving now, it's very convenient to connect Online, WhatsApp or mobile through a video call.

Communication is a two-way road, and I always like to maintain an open line of communication with my mentees. This has helped me listen to their thoughts & have always been available for contact and communicate in an open and friendly manner. This has actually paid off as mentees & my colleagues felt more invested in their work and were motivated to produce greater outcomes, which is the purpose of the mentorship. Each mentee must have their own career, and they should be confident and capable enough to do that. As a mentor, I have avoided coddling with them. The choices in their career must be their own.

I always like to engage in face-to-face conversation to the extent possible to understand body language, facial expressions and emotions which play an influential role in understanding the mentee's true intent. You cannot expect a mentee to open in first conversation because one would like to judge the mentor too before he/she shares.

Remember a Mentor is always considered above parents and peers because sharing is always very personal, and you must give time to your mentee. Mentees must be in the driver's seat and list down their goals that they wish to achieve with the mentor's help. Together, they must create a plan listing short-term, long-term goals and agree on a timeframe to achieve them.

Peter Drucker suggests a particularly important insight from his book, “The Effective Executive”, that “The action plan is a statement of intentions rather than a commitment. It must not become a straitjacket. It should be revised often because every success creates new opportunities”.

Mentees must apply first principles thinking to explore beyond your self-imposed limitations and inversion mental model to switch your brain from a normal way of thinking to the one that will give you the answers to move forward. A Mentor must appreciate mentee even when they make small progress but do not hesitate to criticise the behaviour and the choices. Encourage them to do more, better because the journey itself is the reward.

I have always believed the mentor mentee relationship does not end once the mentee achieves their desired goals. The deep bond formed during these years must last forever. People remember good mentors and mentees throughout their life. They cite their examples when talking to others and draw inspiration from them when faced with challenging circumstances. Their paths may go separate ways, but it is the journey that stays with them forever.

There is no denying that mentoring is an incredibly valuable experience essential for growth and development. "Setting up the right mentor mentee relationship involves creating a safe and supportive environment where both mentor and mentee can engage in building trust, setting goals and achieving them through creative problem solving and solutioning." Peter Drucker

While mentor mentee is a relationship in which one cannot exist without the other, there is a clear separation between their roles.

Let us learn about their roles before developing an effective strategy for this relationship.

A Mentor mentee relationship built out of personal connection and mutual respect. Much like cultivating a land, cultivating a relationship takes time as it requires building trust and aligning with each other's values.

Remember, good mentees can become successful mentors one day. Do your best to create this beautiful relationship that sows the seeds for many more in the future.

**Prof (Dr) Sanjay M Johri**

# The Mentees Perspective

## Mentor – A Blend of Attention, Affection & Active Association

A fruitful mentoring is done by a person who sees more talent and ability in his/her mentee, than they could see in themselves, and helps bring it out to them.

There are various elements that come into play when a person decides to confide in another for his/her personal/professional growth and development.

The mentor-mentee aspect is totally different level in itself. It involves various factors like trust, accountability, transparency, compassion, and being a great communicator.

As it is rightly said, the mentor-mentee relationship is a two-way street, but sometimes due to unfavourable circumstances in a due course of personal and professional development, mentees lag in making ends meet. And, in such situations, a mentor's ability is often put to the test.

Despite having a congenial personality, not every human tunes well with one another always. We all have our own set of short-comings, limitations, past-experiences shaping our psychological behaviour.

Deciding to become a mentor for someone is a life-changing experience. There are quite a few unsaid factors that play a major role in guiding a person into becoming a successful and most importantly a contented human being.

Simply, guiding a mentee for his/her professional growth is not just enough because life solely doesn't revolve around what happens to you. It is more about how you react to what is happening around you. And an experienced mentor has the ability to fix and shape that 'reactive' mode prior to other modes.

Here are a few 'said' elements to look for in a mentor.

**Transparency**

It is vital for a mentee to firmly acknowledge that a mentor holds a great level of transparency in all sense - professional performance growth, career line development, an honest approach in highlighting the strengths and weaknesses of the mentee, aligning the do-able or realistic goals based on the mentee's capabilities, and clearing the air in case of any falsely interpreted notions in any regard. In fact, it's also very important for a mentor to be straightforward about his/her mentee's overall approach in terms of attitude, behaviour, and perception shifts in due course of time.

**Accountability**

A great level of transparency from both ends also leads to the accountability angle. It isn't necessary that the process of growth, paradigm or narrative shift yield positive or desired results each time. Some changes could be just a result of an experimental phase but sometimes things could be down south. So, each party needs to stand accountable for all the happenings; majorly, the mentor needs to understand, accept, and brace for an impact - to keep the spirit held high and motivate the mentee back on track.

**Advocacy**

At times, if situations permits/demand, a mentor can bring the right opportunity straight to the table for his/her mentee to grab, but he would never be able to do a right job on their behalf. And this is where the background mentoring - timely and right advocacy comes into action.

A mentor should be a great advocate for ample success instances, especially the one which have prolonged struggling periods. In fact, advocacy around everything that leads to righteousness, persistence, a focused yet smart career and personal development is a must.

**Availability**

It is a major sense of relief for a mentee to know that his/her mentor will be there in all dire situations. Based on my experience, mentoring never stops. It isn't time-bound unless a mentee is nocturnal and chooses to ping his/her mentor only at human sleeping hours/odd times!

Apart from that, it's vital for a mentee to have a sense of relief, his/her mentor will get back at the earliest possible time.

**Active engagement**

The Mentor needs to engage or participate actively in all the processes or experimental phases his/her mentor is going through - and it could be both professional and personal development. In fact, wherever possible mentors also need to keep track of the performance of mentees when they are being involved at a first-hand industry experience level. The check back with the subordinates at their mentee's workplace could give a better insight into their strengths and weaknesses to work on.

### Compassionate and all ears when in need

This is among the most important aspects of a mentoring relationship, though undoubtedly, it must be both ways. Keeping in mind the mentee's point of view, it's a big emotional support to have someone patiently listen to you through the thick and thin. There are times in our lives when we need someone to patiently listen to us, maybe not provide us with instant solutions, but just be present. In fact, having a compassionate, empathic, all ears' mentors could even save us from falling into the hands of people who tend to feed on other shortcomings and take opportunities instead.

### Constructive criticism

This in fact, comes above everything else, I believe. A true mentor has this trick up his/her sleeves - to be a constant constructive critic. There are times when mentees might find themselves at a complete saturation point, where the feeling of being an overachiever might settle in. And this is the point where a mentor needs to step in to knock that idea down while keeping the spirit high. A mentor needs to sit his/her mentee down from time to time to sink them into a self-analysis stage - how far have they come, where do they currently stand, where do they want to go, while keeping the healthy competition around.

### Provide opportunities and push

It is also expected that a mentor would be able to provide some 'stepping-stone' opportunities and recommendations through his/her established network. But not to forget, it also comes with a high price. Simply being in a mentoring relationship doesn't guarantee this aspect; rather it has to be earned in due course of rigorous time and by proving him/herself a deserving candidate to gain that entitlement.

Once if a mentee is worth giving a shot, then it is expected that the mentor would be willing to roll up his/her sleeves and throw a ball in the mentee's court.

**Great communicator**

Mentoring relationships are primarily based on excellent and clear communication skills. Again, it's a two-way street. Sometimes the mentor needs to take a few more steps to initiate the communication process, but once the flow has been established, then both parties need to be in sync with each other in terms of communication. From time to time, it is necessary for the mentor to sit down with the mentee, and openly communicate with them on agendas which are bugging them up.

**Always maintain confidentiality**

No relationship sustains without a certain level of maintained confidentiality. According to the Maslow Hierarchy, humans need a sense of belonging - they need someone to confide in, and how beautiful it would be to find that person in a mentor. A person who willingly wishes to be a part of your overall journey in terms of professional and personal growth. A mentoring relationship offers a non-biased or non-judgemental response to any circumstances happening in a mentee's life. Therefore, it is also expected that the mentor would withstand all preconceived notions and would aim to contribute to the journey of nurturing his/her mentee with confidentiality.

**Punyja Singh**

# Mentoring

## Caring beyond education and career- By Ratan Mani Lal

Mentoring as an idea in India is of recent origin, and it may not be wholly correct to say it is akin to the *Guru-Shishya Parampara*. The relationship between a mentor and a mentee is not the same as that between a *Guru* and a *Shishya*. In the west, the mentor ceases to be the mentor after the mentee graduates and sometimes, the mentor gives competition to their former mentee. In the east, the relationship often remains sacrosanct. Like a *Guru* who always remains a *Guru* and is often given a higher pedestal than God. This honour may not be there for a mentor.

In the last two or three decades, as there have been many reforms in secondary, technical and higher education, the concept of mentoring as a structured system was introduced in many institutions. This has proved to be so popular and useful that there is often a demand to make it mandatory across educational institutions.

However, it needs to be remembered that a mentor or a mentee may not always be in a position to choose their mentee/mentor. Very often, I have seen the unlikeliest of students become steadfast mentees of equally unlikely teachers. For instance, a teacher in a university or college may be initially lukewarm towards a particular student, but over a period of time, may notice certain traits in the student and then decide to advise, chide and guide that student. At a certain point of time, the student may accept that teacher as a mentor, and such a relationship endures for life. It is significant to note that the mentor may have nothing to gain except to see that the mentee is protected and guided into succeeding in his efforts.

Mentoring for the specific purpose of learning in an institution and choosing the right career could be, in my opinion, a narrow view of the mentor-mentee relationship. Having spent some years in an educational institution gave me an opportunity to interact with hundreds of students over a period of time. However, my decision to return to the industry may not have made me a teacher for life, but I did indeed become a mentor for many of those students. For them, I could do little as far as their career was concerned, but they have remained connected to me for other reasons and consider me a mentor. Often, I wonder, why?

***

At the educational institution level, the student goes simply by what the teacher says because they know little about the subjects being taught. Subsequently, as they begin to analyse what the teacher is trying to teach them, the student learns quickly enough to reach the level of the teacher and often surpasses the teacher. Such students clearly do not feel the need for a mentor. The compulsory mentor-mentee system – if and when mandated – may come as an unnecessary hinderance to such students.

On the other hand, there are students who call up their former teachers on Teachers Day and convey their greetings. They make it a point to reiterate that they remember the teacher because of the bond of trust between them. If a teacher does not treat students as mere learning individuals expected to produce papers and write answer-sheets, but is genuinely interested in their reaching professional heights, each according to their innate ability, then this is a clear mentor-mentee relationship, established organically.

Undoubtedly, the mentor-mentee relationship is something special; it's based on trust and transparency and expects nothing in return. In real life, however, every investment yields returns, some high and some low. But it cannot be so in the case of a mentor-mentee equation, as benevolence and goodwill cannot be measured. I have such relationships with dozens of my former students even though I stopped being their teacher and exited the world of academics decades ago, and now I am neither heading any organisation nor holding any post of eminence. But they (these students) still consider me their mentor and call me up whenever they face any problems which their immediate family members (spouses included), bosses in the office or friends cannot tackle.

***

My friends in academics say that the current system of mentor-mentee relationship in current higher education system especially in the Indian universities entails the mentor to protect the mentee from any imminent danger by giving proper advice and nurturing his/her growth personally and professionally. It is said that it could be important for a mentee to find a mentor who can guide and lead him/her towards success amidst the present complexities of life and career.

I wonder if a mentee can ever have the luxury of choosing a mentor, since a good teacher, a kind person, or a practical senior can rarely be rolled into one; and if it turns out to be so, then that person would be the first choice to be a mentor for dozens or more students.

I believe that a teacher, when embarking on mentorship, needs to look for more than academic mettle in a student. For, in my years of experience, I saw many students who were less serious in classroom studies and more fun-loving than others, later turning out be more worldly-wise where career was concerned. Having noticed their streak of getting test work done or a practical task accomplished rather than exhibiting a penchant for classroom discipline, I just guided them to be a little more attentive towards their studies, and not appear judgemental about their non-academic antics.

These are the students who still consider me their mentor, despite there not being a conscious decision on the part of either of us to choose the other as mentor or mentee. This is, again in my opinion, more to do with a natural inclination to look for talent that is overshadowed by a conscious or sub-conscious streak of rebellion.

There is no denying the fact that a student in modern times – guided and misguided by technology, distracted by an ocean of information, goaded to distrust everyone, and vulnerable because of an inability to choose between right and wrong – faces situations where the advice coming to him/her is more likely to be coloured by the views of the person giving the advice. In such a situation, a mentor in true sense would be that person who accepts the student's dilemma, shares his/her concerns and coaxes him/her to do the best under the circumstances.

As very aptly mentioned elsewhere in this book, the Covid-19 pandemic caused a havoc in the world that is having its ripple effects even more than two years later. The conventional means of education suddenly ceased to exist and, in its place, came a situation for which no one was prepared. Threat to one's survival, dealing with medical emergencies, financial and other crises, and trauma of unimagined proportions changed everything in almost every household. In such a situation, a mentor had to play the role of counsellor as well since so much was at stake.

Mandated mentoring may not have been of much use here, since the mentor himself would be facing similar challenges in life. This can be considered the most suitable situation in which mentoring can be defined. The mentor had to help the mentee get over his/her fears, regain and retain focus on the future, and keep doing whatever was expected by the call of humanity at the moment.

A mentor, in my opinion, is much more than a career guide. He is more of a life coach with a distinctive inclination to shape the mentee's career in such a manner that he/she becomes better equipped to face life's challenges. Such a mentor should always occupy a special place in the life of the mentee. And there is no need to even compare the stature of the mentor's place vis-à-vis the mentee's parents, guardians or idols.

***

Today I look back and wonder: there were many students whose careers were shaped by me, and they moved on. I doubt if they remember those days or even consider me as their mentor. Rather, they would be thinking that I did so because I was paid for doing this. They won't be wrong, though, but then I too may not consider them as my mentees or myself as their mentor.

My mentee would be the one who realised that at that moment in the past, when he/she needed some really relevant and solid advice, it came from me. And then he/she continued to fill me in with the progress in their lives, regardless of the career they chose. Some are living happily as homemakers after working for a few years, while some are in entirely different professions. The urge in them to seek me out was matched by my interest in guiding them, and I thought they really wanted my guidance.

It is true that "Who are we to decide who deserves charity," but mentoring is not charity. It needs to be given to those who are unequivocal about its intentions and willing to be recipients. A secret donation (*gupt daan*) may have its place in the world, but there is nothing like "secret mentoring." Be it traditional one-on-one mentoring, distance mentoring, or group mentoring, it has to be a two-way situation.

I remember my association with Sanjay Mohan Johri, the writer of this book. Though he was not strictly my student, the association was more than that of professional colleagues between us. A science background and science communication were common factors, and later he most helpfully agreed to join me when I started an academic programme in an institute. We both learnt a lot from each other and stood by each other in difficult situations. The relationship of a mentor and mentee between us applies as far as guiding and learning as a two-way situation is concerned. It is overwhelming for me that he considers me as his mentor.

Facing life's challenges and emerging successful needs a lot of ingredients. Hard work, passion, vision, friends, money, co-travellers, cool headedness are some of them. In modern-day success stories, such as start-ups, the idea often comes to the protagonist by simple observation or seeing life's irrationalities from up-close. But the mentor's role could be that of inspiring, consoling and guiding in certain moments. Mentorship, thus, may not be confined to education and career alone – it may extend well beyond this. Both the mentor and the mentee would do well to remember this.

=

*The writer is a senior journalist, editor and commentator.*

## He polished stones into jewels much like his name- Prof Chander Mahadev

When I met Mr. Johri (not Dr. at that point in time) for the first time, as he assumed the mantle of Director at the Amity School of Communication (ASCO) there was an air of heady anticipation. Here I was, an Assistant Professor or maybe a professor in waiting summoned to the Director's chamber. I was a little apprehensive if not cagey about his style of leadership and my style of thinking as the new head of a media institute.

I must have been his senior by 10 years, and he was known to me as a hotshot Science journalist working for the Press Trust of India (PTI). He then turned to media academics, working under the tutelage of my former TOI colleague R M Lal at the Jaipuria Institute of Mass Communication. I would often meet Mr Lal for a possible opening in academics but only formally interacted with Mr Johri since he looked up to Mr Lal as his mentor and since I was RML's former colleague, he too gave me the same respect (deservedly or undeservedly depending on how you look at it.) Even at ASCO, I was technically his senior since I had joined in 2006 and he assumed office sometime in 2009-10.

His seemingly strict and disciplined demeanour as compared to my free-flowing approach with students and how I thought I would shape them into skilled professionals, were a study in contrast. Our first meeting went off somewhat icily if not formally.

We eased into our new relationship and soon struck up a workable, if not affable relationship. Soon after, during one of the expert lectures organized by Mr. Johri and the university big-wigs, I was deeply struck by a pithy remark made by the highly impressive academic Dr. Bhoomittra Dev, former Vice-Chancellor of Gorakhpur University, who articulately explained that a true mentor is like a milestone, without whom a student (a mentee) will lose his way, but once he is on the road to skilful professionalism, he should leave the mentor far behind, like the milestone he encountered in the first place. This set me thinking and without ever thanking Dr. Dev for this brilliant insight, I realised that this is the path I will forthwith follow in my quest to empower students.

Soon after, both Mr. Johri and I started chalking out an action plan to ensure students learn the difference between a degree and a skill. Both of us were from the industry and knew that the skill gap we were encountering in our students was too wide to be bridged through either an internship or through special classes. We both then started holding special exposure sessions and workshops wherein students were given first hand exposure to working in a news agency, a newspaper or a News Channel.

I would often make it a point to tell my final year students that they were unpolished gems, and it was the professor's or faculty's job to polish them into diamonds or jewels, not knowing that the director himself was a Johri (a jeweller) even by name. It was at this point in time that Amity University came up with a Mentee-mentor programme wherein each faculty had to take under his/her wings at least 10-15 students and ensure they remained mentees till they passed out of ASCO. By now, Mr. Johri was Dr. Johri, and he took upon this task with all sincerity and aplomb. He also gave his mentees professional reporting assignments and even set up a website for them to post their stories and get his feedback. The two of us along with Dr

Areena Mirza then organized annual media festivals like Via Media, Event Management festivals, TV News Symposia, Photography contests and it was he who spread it across the university spanning different disciplines. Dr. Johri also helmed and headed the Amity University house journal and organized essay and poetry competitions. By now, he had become the most popular HOD on campus. By the year 2016, I left ASCO for greener pastures and Dr. Johri continues to burn the proverbial midnight lamp by polishing his students into jewels, and today he has a book titled "With Love, Sir" under his belt. I am on my part, reminded of the iconic Sydney Poitier Film, To Sir, with love. Keep on keeping on, Dr. Johri, differences notwithstanding. Since today happens to be Krishna Janmashthami, I would say the Sanathan Sarathi continues to create gems albeit in his own style.

Prof. Mahadev is Communication Specialist, Lead Trainer, Writer & pedagogue

## 'A mentor who vouches to stick till the last'

Luckily, it wasn't my nose landing when I joined Amity School of Communications as a bachelor's student at Amity university, Lucknow campus. Though, I do envy my other high school friends who got into other public universities in the state and at other parts of the country because they have had what is called an 'experience' – a bit of ragging session, bunking lectures, delayed assignments, low attendance percentage and all this without facing any significant consequences.

Well as a result, today we might not be trading and reflecting in our lives with an identical perception style! I am not emphasising completely on implying a strict learning atmosphere 'as a sole way' to succeed in life but in my experience so far – adhering to the basics actually shapes an individual for an array of unknown and unexpected challenges in life.

The faculties at Amity school of communication followed those strict guidelines and if I retrace my steps, actually it's the Head of the Institution's responsibility to maintain such guidelines – no doubt Amity is still known for it.

Being a part of mentor-mentee programme has been one of the most rewarding experiences not just in my professional learning aspect but also on psychological well-being aspect of life.

Some of my peers found the practiced guidelines suffocating but on personal level, it kept me on track, check and surprisingly gave me a lot of breathers.

There are times in our life when we find ourselves doing great on external (educational) level but are way behind in terms of understanding our true potential. We tend to face the people on the outside but fail to learn about ourselves from the inside.

Mentor-mentee programme actually bridges that gap of learning about oneself from inside out before stepping in the real world.

During the time of pandemic, Sir had a thought of writing a book on the significance and impact of mentor-mentee programme. In fact, he shared with me his entire plot, style, approach for the book, and offered me an opportunity to contribute to whatever extend I could do based on my acquired editorial skills.

Initially, I was quite a bit jittery about my potential of being able to contribute anything for a book that is being written by the Head of the Institution of a university/my mentor.

But gradually, after thoroughly understanding the clear concepts and requirement of his book, I gathered my thoughts and started doing some literature review/research about the mentor-mentee book writing styles.

Over the period of good six months, my experience of working on the collected testimonials actually enriched my perception about mentor-mentee relationship/programme to a great extend!

To my surprise, the significance and impact of a mentor remains on his/her mentee for a lifetime, and the legacy carries on.

The mentee doesn't only develop professionally but also realises the importance of self-awareness, deep-rooted potentials, limitations and most importantly psychological well-being.

These elements also help an individual in nurturing his/her surrounding in the best possible favourable working atmosphere which further leads to an excellent performance both in their professional and in personal life.

In my experience so far through this book, I learned the importance and value of having a mentor who vouches to stick till last; and the intensity of impact he/she creates on his/her mentees' both on professional and personal level.

I believe putting it in a bit technical term - the concept of this book has set an exemplary example on mentor-mentee relationship/programmes' impact, monitoring and evaluation aspect.

As a matter of fact, in the time span of three years of my bachelor's course, the institution offered plethora of opportunities. Generally, students who are upfront and expressive in nature often get noticed by the faculties and are given the platform to present their skills. But unfortunately, the introvert, shy, low-esteemed are often left behind. And to quite an extend its fair too because no one has the time to fish you out and then gamble on you!

Furthermore, if one doesn't have the ability to showcase or market him/herself while simultaneously aspires to excel in the field of mass communication – I believe, these two aspects don't fit in a box.

Regrettably, I happen to be the 'latter' one, but as far as the working norms are concerned, I rather turned out as a fortunate one. Honestly, apart from your parents all it takes is just one 'experience-based analyses' of your potential by an extraordinarily experienced professional – in a setting of a right institute which can offer equal opportunities to further develop.

This might sound difficult to digest but the same analyst wouldn't meet you in all your glory but in fact, could give you 'tuff times' and could be an intense critic.

I don't recall any of my faculty applauding and speaking high of me in three years course of my bachelors'. Rather I sensed myself living under tight scrutiny and radar for the first three semesters!

In fact, I had no faculty pin-pointed from whom I could fetch descent grades by fluke primarily based on face-value. All that ever spoke for me was my work and a bit of a good gesture maybe!

It's bit rare for a mentor to deliberately hand-pick the 'latter' ones, and work with them continuously after the completion of a course under their guidance as a professor. And this is the point where that mentor/faculty is no more liable to your academic progress, assignment attributions or anything that has to do with your life.

In spite of being free from all this still if he/she decides to stick with you and guides you in your professional life, listens, senses the fear, ambiguity and accordingly advices in your life saving decision making skills – then believe me you have been fished out and to quite an extend they won their gamble on you!

As mentioned, despite being the 'latter' one, during my bachelor's my mentor Dr. (Prof.) Johri silently hand-picked me and always tested in hot waters. Through him I got an opportunity to be a part of a week-long workshop that took place in Amity Noida campus.

It turned out as a bubble-bust moment for me which made me realise I actually have chosen to trade in unknown waters – by choosing mass communication! I got an opportunity to learn the incompetent part of myself and further work on them.

In that workshop, I could never gather the guts to step up and play a role of newsreader in the Noida campus studio despite knowing that I certainly would have made plenty of mistakes but definitely not those ones which then my friends made on screen.

A year later while perusing my masters in Melbourne when I sensed an opportunity to read a weather report via teleprompter, believe me I jumped out of my seat, walked out of the production control room and silently stood next to my professor in the studio. After a couple of practise sessions, a final shot was taken which surprisingly impressed him!

Actually, it wasn't a big of a deal to anyone present in that room but for me I swam across an English Channel!

I could have remained seated like last year and then later would have regretted by re-playing that moment repetitively in my mind – Had I been in his/her position, I could have read it like this, or I could have presented it with better voice modulation and expressions.

So, had I not got an opportunity by my mentor at Amity, I never would have known this incompetency of mine and unknowingly it must have stayed with me forever, and have reflected in my style of working too.

Undoubtedly, either it would have crippled me to sense such opportunity ahead in my life or given it my first timer - I would have messed it up then.

Something similar happened when my mentor Mr. Johri gave me another opportunity of being a 'curator' in a university's event. I guess it was his style of testing or encouraging my self-confidence/existing potential.

I was given a time frame of just few hours to create an anchor's profile of an event' guests. It was challenging but that actually gave me a boost about my working under pressure skills – I realised if I am designed to mess thing up a couple of times then with some major rectifications, I can try my best to deliver the desired results in a time-bound conditions, because I have done it earlier.

To my shock, he was also the internal invigilator for my major final year project! I actually had given up my hopes to score any descent grade and was ready to face the strict evaluation. I still remember, out of fear and hopelessness, I finished my project way before time but sat on it for few days just not to raise any plagiarism concern.

On final day, yet few days prior to the deadline, I walked into his cabin to submit my hardcopy. I had my fingers crossed and prayed not to encounter him seated but rather it looked as if he had been waiting for my appearance to submit my project. Within a blink of an eye, I was out of his hair – I didn't just vanish from his cabin but from the adjoining waiting area too!

I only wished for passing grades then, but I actually scored grade nine! It was the time when I realised that with right focus on my work (without any expectations), I might be able to do something well with my career.

Honestly, I hate being moved out of my cocoon and giving surprise tests, but life isn't fair to anyone, I guess!

My mentee and mentor relationship with Prof. (Dr.) Johri actually began when it was time for me to leave Amity. For my masters' education, I got admission in Australia. Though I had a lot of unclarity in mind about it, but I decided to stick with it as I am the 'latter' one – inexpressive or non-communicative.

To my surprise, Sir Johri actually sensed my ambiguity, and he shared his heartfelt experience when his eldest daughter left for her graduation to United Kingdom – about her struggles, experiences and opportunities.

He also cleared my doubts on why students opt for part-time jobs and there is no shame in doing a non-white-collar job to make some money as long as it doesn't affect your studies.

Perhaps, like a 'protective father' he exclusively guided me further about the open-society culture of western countries – the importance of staying grounded with your roots, apart from having an exploration itch for a new country also have greater concentration on studies because at the end of a day, that's what you would there be for!

Less did he know that I would take this advice as a bait and followed it religiously because given my basic instincts of being highly introvert; I found comfort in restricting my trips from my university's residence to the library at the most.

I admit this advice actually kept me quite focused and so much over the top of my assignments that for a couple of times my faculties gave extra attention to my submissions for uploading them way too ahead from the rest of my classmates! They also doubted me once for plagiarism and ran specific checks on my submitted assignments; thankfully their results always came lower than what I indicated through my software!

Anyway, by the completion of my two-year masters' course, I actually had a sense of stark realization that I never explored even the much accessible part of the country. Forget about my friends even my father explored Melbourne ten times more than me in his mere ten days' vacation!

However, I don't have regrets because I may have explored a lot all, but I know almost all the beautiful and accessible state & public libraries of Melbourne city, lesser-known creeks to clear the head in solitude, the most comfortable and electrically powered nooks and corners of my university to hide from people, aromatic yet strong coffee for better concentration, and how and when to secure a cheap deal on shopping!

Honestly, apart from keeping myself focused, this advice of Sir Johri actually helped me to saved quite a lot of money; and yes, as the advice goes, I unresistingly took up the first part-time job opportunity I got to add some more to my savings! Though, the part-time experience taught me a lot about time-management skills, how to be diplomatic, stay calm and deal with the nuisance of working under someone who runs a business based on 'mere profit.'

So, actually all it depends on how seriously and in what direction one takes the given advice. And eventually humans are designed to incline more towards what they are comfortable with or already unconsciously interested in.

Perhaps, for me this turned out as descent win-win situation - I managed to maintain good grades and not just had practical learning on the importance of saving money rather adding more to it with good time-management skills.

It's bit unique for a mentor to check back on their mentees once they walk out with a degree from the university. To anyone's surprise, I suppose, Sir Johri always trace back his mentees and keep a track of them all.

In fact, it was quite a heartfelt gesture of Sir Johri to bid a goodbye by paying me a visit at my place, a day before I had to leave India to continue my ongoing masters in Australia. And not to forget from that day onwards my grandmother and my parents got an assurance that the achieved grades in my graduation's marksheet are trust-worthy and a result of my hard-work!

As mentioned about my basic instincts of being an introvert (which I am still working on) Sir Johri always filled in the gaps. He kept checking back on me and in fact, guided me about the existing industry-based opportunities based on my developing interest and potential.

So, based on my experience so far, the mentor-mentee relationship isn't always restricted till one is enrolled as a professor or student in an institution.

It often goes beyond and if the chosen mentees are lucky enough, they would definitely find themselves being tested in hot waters at all the times. But trust me you might run out of luck at times but under the guidance of such a mentor you would never run out of an optimistic and experienced-based practical advice to navigate your way out per se.

A heartful thank you for shaping me into what I am today and for your constant acceptance of what and who I am as a person.

With Love, Sir,

Punyja Singh

Media Advisor Economic Media Centre Melbourne (Australia)

***Comments***

*There are very few students with whom you stay in constant touch during, and after your studies. Relationships are shared by many people, but the depth of the relationship is always mutual as it depends on both the parties.*

*In the 22 years of journalism so far, I have seen a different way of understanding relationships, especially among girls. It is also true that a girl takes a longer time to decide whether the person in front is you is a well-wisher or not!*

*Punyja was one such a gentle & pious girl! She has always been a topper in her studies, but she took a lot of time to decide on her career.*

*A little reserved by nature, she used to talk only as much as it was needed, perhaps she was also testing whether the person in front of her deserve a relationship of Mentor!*

*Her father was already abroad & parents focus for the two daughters was to ensure that they complete their master's from abroad, and she moved to Australia.*

*I would describe my relationship with her as a very special, and quite intimate perhaps beyond Mentor-Mentee as we both kept in constant touch via email & phones. Yes, I did help her for couple of internships she did with the industry & I am happy wherever she worked she left a mark!*

*Her writing skills were amazing, and I remembered that! During her stay in India at the time of the pandemic, I thought why not plan something different, and thus we entered in an alliance & come out with a book on Mentoring.*

*This however came as a big surprise for her, but I was firm on my decision that this was the right opportunity to hone her craft!*

---

## A guide who prepared me to face challenges

Sir, I believe everything that you have taught me in class has also guided me about the outside world too. These learnings have helped me to make choices more wisely. You once told me to not burden my thoughts with the future too much, and I think this one simple thought helps me cope with different difficulties.

The most unconventional personal and professional decision for me was not to pursue masters' studies rather work after my bachelors.

When I you about my choice, you were supportive of my choice and your words of encouragement always helps me through difficult times. Especially in one instance, when I was working as a copywriter and my copies were getting rejected. The rejection was new to me, and I was starting to get annoyed and disheartened.

Then, I would remember if my teacher, my mentor and a man so capable with words have always believed in my skill, there must be something inside that is worth the praise and I need to channel that. I believe your boundless support in me always helps me move past writer's blocks and rejections.

In fact, there are times when one can feel intimidated to share concerns with a senior member, especially the head of the department of the university. But in this case, you always had and still have an open-door policy.

Whether it was your classes that opened a daily interaction gateway between freshers and you, or one sharing his/her concern. I have personally always been able to voice out my opinions freely with you.

To name an event, would be to go to the very beginning and recall my discomfort during Freshers. I didn't want to stand out or even participate in the ceremony, but you convinced me that this would be for my betterment while also promising to consider my discomfort. Another instance, I would like to recall would be during the pandemic, when I felt disheartened with the academic shift, you were there to lend an ear.

Thank you, Sir for hearing me out in the hour of need.

With love, Sir

Adeeba Lari

**Social Media Strategist and Copy Writer (Freelance)**

***Comments.***

*The girl from industrial town Kanpur was bit reserved initially and took time to settle down. As a Print Faculty, I always test a student through assignments and Adeeba looked promising. Her content skills were strong though but at times were more fictional.*

*Coming from a traditional Muslim family, I recall she was quite hesitant to participate in freshers on stage, and went in conversation whether it would be appropriate? But later she got convinced that nothing is wrong to be open if she aspires to grow professionally. I am glad, she did not look back since that day.*

*From 'Class representative' she became darling of everyone in the institution. Won awards and represented institution in every event. She developed herself with great research aptitude and hogged the limelight. She laid strong foundation for the University Digital Club and worked for three years of course.*

*Whenever I asked, 'What is next in plans?', the cool girl always said, 'Sir, I like to take things at gradual pace.' She moved on and today holds an important position in the company. Abeeba is someone who will be in my thoughts always.*

## “A mentor with an open-door policy irrespective of any situation.”

The best thing for students in Amity School of communications has been ‘You, Sir.’

You have always been available to help in department. In fact, from the day one, you encourage your students to interact with you about any concerns that they may have. When the head of the department has such an open-door policy, the new students who have come to a new environment feel very comfortable.

There have been several instances over the two years where I have shared many issues and experiences, but I will tell two of them. The first one was in my first year just within ten days, I joined Masters in Journalism and Mass Communication.

I was nervous and had an exam coming up for which I needed to leave for few days for my preparations. I discussed this with other faculty members, but they said that I won’t be able to get leave for such a long period. Luckily, when I discussed the same with you, I got some leverage time to prepare from my exams. It has been one of the most helpful things in that situation.

The second instance was later, I was confused about my future and things which I could do after my masters. I discussed it with you and since then till today you have been really concerned about my career, suggesting me various opportunities which has been very helpful.

In my 2 years at Amity and even later you have always been very kind to me. Even when you have been critical it has been like fatherly feedback.

You have done a lot for me in my 2 years which I will always be grateful and never forget. You have always appreciated me of my work but when you have been critical it has always helped me to reflect of my work and has rather made me better.

You always encouraged me to do things which I being shy and reserved would have never done before. Helped me to grow not just being a better writer, but also its because of him I am more confident in life.

Thank you, Sir, for being my guardian angel and helping me through out!

With love, Sir

Aman

Independent Journalist

***Comments***

*Hardcore in academics, Aman's entry into the institution will be remembered as a Shy & introvert boy whose father was always concerned about his introvert attitude. Certainly, being the single child, he was pampered. Though, he preferred to be the backbencher, and always paid attention to the lectures.*

*He had depth and political writing was his forte. Six months into the studies, I could spot him shifting to the front benches. He realised the need to push his limits, and then he finished his course as Topper with a Gold Medal!*

*He changed and developed as a Political Analyst. What a transformation and our success to take best out of him.*

## “A changemaker who helped me fight to choose right path'

Well firstly, I would not be here and sharing my thoughts if it had not been you.

I learnt to fight, to choose the right and make the best of what you have and to be the change if you want to see the change. So much so I firmly believe that deep down I chose Amity and am immensely proud of it. I will never barter it for anything. This is the spirit instilled in me by you and the institution.

You have been the change maker, the knight in shining armour for the students of ASCO and ever since nothing has been the same. Our institute became the go to college for all aspiring youth for education whose parents were sceptical about sending them away.

You gave the department the fresh air of practicality, solidarity, kinship, and team spirit. One thing that I learnt from you was that if you want to change anything and really see the change start by setting examples and the first step to do is by doing it yourself.

Second, to really want things to happen, you have to make it happen and the best way to do it is by learning to unlearn, understand, innovate, and educate. Soon you as our mentor got into everything and understanding things and BAM!! We started to see what you wanted us to see. This taught me that our actions are everything. ‘One is not a man of his/her own words until one act upon it.’

Soon the ASCO department was the living proof of things we only talked about, things in black & white translated into actions, better faculty, better facilities, more exposure. We had clubs so that each student can hone their skills and passions as much attention was paid on curriculars,

I believe that the young aspiring media person needed more than just textbook knowledge, you gave a lot of attention to the extracurricular activities too, organized media summits, field trips, practical assignments, and projects.

You also allowed us to participate in various inter college competitions. They were made to do with what you have and use the little resources you have. So, we started a small ASCO's Thought Cafe on a college board. We soon were publishing our ASCO newsletter, there were photo exhibitions and wherever there were events in other departments we were sent to take up the responsibility just like 1st hand experience for a newbie event manager.

You were the only H.O.D I have known who knew his students by their names and have always been available to help them. Soon, ASCO and you had conquered the entire Amity. That's when I realized the importance of my course that anything that can be documented is news, anything that is happening in and around is an event. That is the power we vested in ourselves when we took this course, and you made us believe this and in ourselves too.

All this might be sounding so glorious. That's where my last learning comes from, the change maker taught us that only sincere dedication, determination, constant effort, patience, hard work, good work ethics and honesty can take you anywhere you want to and slowly is the fastest way to reach wherever you want to go and be.

It's been 10 years ever since I left Lucknow and have made a decent life in Mumbai - The city of dreams. I try to follow and live by the thing I wrote above, and it is because you as my mentor instilled in me not just in words and writing but by showing us all those things happen when we act on it.

In fact, you taught me to be practical and be action oriented and never slack or be complacent in life. You also insisted on the fact that the comfort zone is human's biggest enemy, and one should always keep reinventing and innovating.

Lastly, I would like to end by saying that you have been strict but approachable and I congratulate each & every student that they got a chance to be mentored by you.

You are always there for your students – one just has to ask for your help, and you are there.

With love Sir,

Ambika Chandra

Creative Producer

***Comments***

*I got to know about Ambika only at the far end of her second year of bachelor's because I joined the university around that time, and the students were then new to me. The institution entered into a major partnership with UNICEF in 2009-2010 for 3-days Child Rights Summit.*

*Actually, this partnership opened opportunities for students of her batch to showcase their talent in - photography, filmmaking and organizing an event to a different scale since UNICEF's expectation from an educational institution were high. From photography to visualization and scripting Ambika came up with an amazing talent and perhaps this was the time she realized her capabilities.*

*Always cool and thoughtful, I knew what she had in store and when I decided to do a documentary on the life of Elderly People, Ambika was the perfect choice for the background research and scripting. "Shaam Huyi Hai" was released by top cop Ms. Kiran Bedi former Governor Pondicherry (Union Territory).*

## 'A mentor & a fatherly figure who always stood by my side'

*("The Alchemist possesses the art of gilding but only a Goldsmith can scratch gold from the darkest mines.")*

The majority of the learnings come from a person who is not just a mentor but a father like figure, who never left my side. Someone, whom I can never really forget, and owns a big place in my heart and mind. He is no one other than you, Sir.

As an aspiring communication student, I always wanted to become an anchor and there is one such event where I showcased my talent. It was a travelogue shoot which had to take place in Mathura.

You approved my audition and was the one who pushed me for the same. In 2 days, I was in Mathura where I had the best 6 days of my life. This travelogue is still loved by people around me and I would give the entire credit to you for the same. If it wasn't for him, I wouldn't have been able to gain this confidence of speaking in front of the camera.

There are a lot of teachings of yours, which can never be replaced. A few of them to mention are-

- Work hard, no matter what.
- Be unique, think unique
- Face your fear and you will succeed (Otherwise, sir will give you such opportunity where you will have to face it. Trust me, it helps!)
- Take out some time in a day to work on yourself
- Keep looking for opportunities to grow
- Sleep less, work more

You have been more like a friend and a father figure to me. You are really open minded and is someone who will try and always show you the path towards light. I have shared a lot of personal issues and experiences with him, one of which was really serious for me and my family. You could sense it even before I had the chance to tell it to you.

Like every other student I have doubted myself too. This doubt, which was certainly followed by demotivation was always cleared up by you. No matter what it was about, you never stayed back from motivating me or to make me think as how I fit this line of career. And showed me the path wherever required and helped me with any kind of issue that I was facing.

It is said that "*हीरे की परख जौहरी ही जानता है, (*only true goldsmith can detect actual gold) which is somewhere true as he is the one who pushed me wherever required. Although, I am not calling myself a diamond, but surely you are a person who can take out the best from a person.

With love, Sir

Amisha Tewari

Account Executive, Wunderman Thompson

***Comments***

*A silent girl always focused on her studies. One could not think Amisha's real talent would come to the surface from the second year of her Graduation. I had been watching her strong writing skills that I always tested in every student, but she perhaps under-estimated herself in the beginning.*

*We always need to push and evoke a sense of realization in them about their capabilities. I was confident she would top, and she did so. In fact, her confidence was boosted post our mentoring, and since then there was no going back.*

*I knew she has a good voice and can anchor. After anchoring in a couple of documentaries her confidence rose to new heights.*

*Some unprecedented crises in the family originated as a disaster, and I thought to give a daily dose with some motivational messages. She stood strong and never compromised with her studies. She completed the course with university's highest honour in academics. In fact, placement was never a problem for Amisha, and after her graduation she went to industry, then further for Masters.*

*Today she is with a top Advertising brand company and her professional journey has begun. Miles to go!*

## 'A man who goes the extra mile to shape a career, and future '

*("Iron sharpens iron, so one man sharpens another"- Bible)*

With perfect integrity, I can admit that you have been that man in my life. Following my passion, in 2014 - I started the journey of knowledge sharing but it was 2016 when I met someone who literally led me a like a shepherd into the academic pastureland. This note is an opportunity to show my humble gratitude and reverence to that "someone" you, Sir.

I knew you as a Head of Institution of my alma mater Amity School of Communication since 2011. I still have a clear memory of you taking my admission interview and asking about the front-page news in newspaper. At that time, I didn't expect you would be my teacher, guide, mentor and boss.

One man played different roles in shaping my career and personality. You have been through thick and thin contributing both on personal and professional front. It gives me immense pleasure to talk about two integral contributions from your side – showing confidence on me when I was nothing and pushing me to dive deep into the sea so that I can learn from mistakes.

In the beginning of my Ph.D. program, I faced few early hiccups and as I said like a good coach you allowed me to go through those challenges, face the heat and make a comeback. This piece will not be absolute if I don't mention about his helping and caring conducts. I cannot forget your attention, counsel and concern for me when I was facing a strenuous medical complication in my family. You were not only guiding me but also comforting a fusspot like me!

With outright sincerity, I would like to acquire few of your qualities – one among them are your man management skills, your head is very clear in extracting the best from an individual.

Secondly but equally important is going extra mile for people. I have witnessed you doing this for people including me. Now that is something which I really admire and want to inculcate in my personality. No matter what people do or say about you. You are there to give best for them.

This is a short journey with you which is still going on. I believe there is lot more to experience and assimilate from you in coming time.

With love, Sir,

Mr. Amit Massey

Assistant Professor, Amity University

***Comments***

*From a PG Student to Mentor, and then colleague - today Amit is a big support to the institution, and we work together. Everyone takes time to understand his role as you grow and take up responsibilities.*

*Amit is a boy who has been steady but consistent and proved himself in the different roles. Popular among students as "Amit Sir", he is one among the "pillars" of the institution.*

*Very emotional at times he feels very low, and I sense it from his face. I like to counsel him, and next day you will find him back with more energy. Over the years he has shown great confidence and maturity and he is a highly disciplined person.*

*Just waiting to address him as Dr. Amit as he draws close to submit his Ph.D.*

## 'The guiding light who paved the right path'

The mentor-mentee program by Amity School of Communication is like a boon for students who seek guidance & direction. I was lucky enough to get you as my mentor, who successfully played many roles at a time.

Yes, content writing was always my passion, but you made me believe that I could actually make a career out of it. Thanks to you, sir. In a real sense, you acted like a mentor for me, guiding me on different walks of life, career-decisions, industry, etc.

The superb initiative by you 'Mentor-Mentee' program has made me realize how important it is to have a guiding light in life and Thank You for becoming one.

From my first content assignment to where I am today, you've actually paved the right path for me. It was always so natural and homely to simply walk in your office and have career-oriented discussions.

Trust me, sir when I say this, there is no HOI I have ever seen who goes out of his way to do so much for his/her students. More than the students, I have seen the enthusiasm in you to make bright careers for not just your mentees but every student.

There is no doubt about it that you have encouraged me to enter in the content industry and become a successful professional. From starting off with little internships, to writing SEO content on different genres at one of my dream companies seems nothing less than a dream. And I am quite sure, you'll always be there for me and your mentees at any point in time.

What would I do if I wasn't given the right opportunities? You gave me those opportunities to flourish and make a successful career out of it.

Thank you for always encouraging me and being an essential part of my professional journey.

With Love, Sir

Anchal Gupta

SEO Lifestyle Writer, The Good Glamm Group

***Comments***

*She entered as a bubbly girl to the Graduation and the best thing about her that she was in the company of some very bright students from the start. All these students were highly competitive, and she moved towards her goal steadily. Institution gets lot of opportunities and sometimes it is difficult to test a student on his/her capabilities. We got one opportunity when I, as a director had to choose one and my vote went to Anchal. She kept up to my expectations and won laurels.*

*A talented student always remains confused to choose career and I knew Anchal would get one of the best because of her multi-talented abilities. She faced tough time in the family too and lost her father in the midst of studies. But she stood firm towards her goals. Salute to her for keeping promise to be one of the best, and she works as senior professional in media industry.*

## 'A mentor who imparted knowledge, life lessons'

(*"Great teachers focus not on compliance, but on connections and relationships." – P.J Caposey)*

I realized it was not just a quote that I would appreciate reading, but a reality that I could relate to, as well.

I had the privilege of learning under your guidance in the year 1998-2000, while I was pursuing Mass Communication from Lucknow University. So much to learn from you, and so much to treasure. Not just education and knowledge, but memories and nostalgia too.

What you always wanted us to gain was, practical knowledge of reporting in journalism. And it really helped us gain immense confidence with the field work that we did under your guidance. Something that is still helping at work, and in life also in general. I strongly believe those were 'life lessons' and not just the curriculum lessons that he imparted back then.

You have a special way of communicating and teaching - with an endearing smile, cracking jokes, sharing knowledge and your own experiences. Something that you carry with you all your life and do not forget once out of the campus. The write ups that he would give us to do, are still in my possession along with his encouraging remarks.

I came to Mumbai in 2000 to make my career in Film and Television Industry. Since then, 20 years in Film production, Tv Programming as a creative and now as a full-time freelance writer, the journey has been really enriching. I am glad that all this while, the 'communication' continued with you, year after year. Probably you are the only mentor I am still in touch with, and it really feels great to be able to seek your advice, share my challenges and achievements with you on time to time.

In today's time, where time is valued as 'time is money' mostly, and everybody is busily running all the time for it, I feel lucky to have you around to helps me to 'pause' and 'talk' and 'listen' and 'share' life's big and small joys and challenges.

With love, Sir

Anju Kapoor

Writer and Lyricist

Formerly Creative Director Colours; Viacom & Sony (Television Programming)

***Comments***

*My association with Anju dates back to 90s when I was working as full-time Journalist with PTI & also teaching at Lucknow University as a Guest Faculty to PG Students pursuing Mass Communication.*

*With no laptops, smartphones and chrome students paid more attention to their faculty, unlike the today's scenario about student's span of attention around plethora of information readily available on tips of fingers.*

*I used all my professional experience in teaching and in every class, I used to teach a subject with a case study and students always enjoyed. I made it a practice to put students to field assignments and Anju, the lanky girl came up with her content. Yes, she had a strong pen.*

*Those were the days when 'placement' opportunities were not arranged as professionally as we do these years. One had to experiment and try hard, and Anju after her initial years of work moved to Mumbai. She struggled hard but was confident about her abilities.*

*Anju has today earned a place in the industry.*

## ‘Your personal stories inspired me to chase my foreign study dreams’

*“A mentor with a concoction of an amazing friend, believer and guide”*

Sir, you have been an excellent and exemplary mentor to me since 2018. Since my bachelor’s degree you have been guiding me in my career and through your informative guidance, I was able to recognize my goal for the future.

You have been in constant touch with me and have always been there to guide and provide contact of your business associates in the industry who further enhanced my practical knowledge and skill set.

After the completion of my bachelor’s degree, based on my interests and skills you helped me in deciding the industry which was best suitable for me. In fact, you also helped me in applying for Universities in UK and USA to pursue my master’s degree; persuaded me to complete online courses and participate in extra-curricular activities to enhance my skills and further enrich my CV.

Actually, your shared experiences and struggles about the past students and your children about fulfilling their dreams to study abroad, inspired me to apply at foreign universities and explore the new opportunities in my career.

If you remember Sir, initially I didn’t get much support from my family, but you stood by me and helped me convinced my family about this decision.

Not to forget, even after flying all the way to UK you have always been in constant touch with me – taking regular updates about my studies and health. You thoroughly understand transitions in the beginning phases of students can be rough and tough on them to deal with.

It's because of you, I have been able to excel in my career and have gained self-confidence to take a stand in my best interest.

I am truly grateful to have such an amazing mentor, who really understands each and every student on a deeper and personal level and guides them accordingly by being an honest and reliable friend!

Thank you, Sir, for being there when I needed you the most.

With love, Sir,

Archana Jagwani

Leeds University, UK

***Comments***

*From a small town Lakhimpur Kheri - 150 km away to Lucknow and then to London! It has been an amazing journey for Archana who was one of the best students in the entire batch, but she probably preferred being in her own group!*

*All the teachers liked her. I observed her silently and could see a spark. Something was different with this girl, and she was meant for foreign studies.*

*Right after her graduation, I asked what your plans are now?*

*And pat came the reply "Sir I am planning to pursue higher studies abroad and am in touch with few consultants about good universities."*

*There was initial opposition in the family as all parents have a fear that how their little daughter will study & stay abroad alone!*

*It was Archana's determination, and her father's support that she is not only completing her Masters in London today but has also moved towards fulfilling her dream.*

*Good Luck Archana.*

## 'You showed me my goal and transformed my life'

More than a decade ago, back in the year 2009, I heard of you as the head of the institution and as a very disciplined individual who had absolute zero tolerance towards non-sense, contrary to which I was full off.

I feel gratified to those non-sensical qualities, some of which I still think I possess, which brought me face-to-face to a mentor, who very seriously once said 'please be serious about your career, as out there stands a world, where there is a cutthroat competition'.

That once scolding from you had a frightening as well as a brightening effect or rather say 'impact' on my life because, I started changing my path every time, I saw you walking and secondly, gave me my life goal which got me completely transformed.

As I sway down the memory lane, somewhere around 2015 when I was in touch with a senior faculty of mine, suggested me to apply for a position at Amity School of Communication to which I was completely reluctant. "Johri Sir would never like to see me as his colleague" was my blunt reply to which he said, you don't know him yet, give it a try. Today, here I am, a completely transformed personality.

You are a super mentor, a brilliant guide, mentor and teacher and last but not the least an extraordinary human being with an exemplary spirit. A spirit of joy, courage, hope, learning and support, the list indefinitely goes on.

Simple using the word 'I thank you, and I admire you' would not do justice to a being who has been with me as a pillar of support, an entity to rely upon and most importantly a boss who stands with you in dire times of need, against all odds. I was, I am, and I'd always be a student of communication when it comes to writing my feelings but trust me nobody is forcing me to stop writing except myself.

Sir, mere saying 'Thank you' won't do justification to your deeds towards non-sensical minds like me. Instead, I'd just say 'All the very best.'

With love

Asha Adhikari

Assistant Professor, Amity University

***Comments***

*A student for her master's program, and then later she was my colleague for well over five years. Asha has a special place for me Down Memory Lane. I never took this girl seriously as often I found her in fun mode 'masti' and looked 'naughtier' during her university days though she graduated with high grades.*

*Maybe it was because I had joined as Director of the institute in the same year then, and my focus was more in building the institution.*

*I learnt more about Asha when she joined me as a colleague, and I decided to groom her into this new role and over the years she grew as a mature faculty though I scolded her whenever she went wrong.*

*She not only earned respect among students but became darling of her colleagues. For me she was always dependable. One of the best quality Asha developed was being cool, and you would never find her irritating. This lanky woman has a great future ahead!*

## 'You helped me move out of my comfort zone, and chase success'

*"2020 marked the end of my journey with Amity School of Communication but your guidance has always been eternal"*

Today if I sit and recall my three years of growth and development, I could say that this roller-coaster ride was impossible without the support and encouragement of my peers. I started as a novice, and I was prepared for the industry in these three years with your support and guidance, Sir.

I still remember myself as an under-confident girl lost in the crowd. There comes my mentor, you, who noticed the spark in me and provided me with ample opportunities to brace me up for the industry. And, as we all know, it always takes two to tango. I made equal attempts to make you proud to trust me and stand by your expectations.

This mentor-mentee relationship has been my primary support that didn't only last till college, but it's still helping me and guiding me through the dark whenever I feel helpless. This bond has always encouraged me to grow and has pushed me out of my comfort zone.

I still remember I was always a shy, off-the-camera girl, but you pushed me to try anchoring which is still not my cup of tea. You asked me to prepare my script and take the responsibility of the stage in one of our college events.

Though I was extremely nervous and wanted to say 'no,' but your confidence in me made me take this bold step to move out of my comfort zone and take risk. That's how we achieve success, right? That day, you made me realize how to chase success, and that's how life has been till now.

Today I am working in an advertising agency as a copywriter, and a whole lot of credits behind this small achievement belongs to this unwavering support that I received from you.

I know I can't return the favour for the guidance and support you have given me throughout, but I can indeed say that my achievements will pay you back, and I will always take this bond forward with me wherever I will go.

Thank you for being my guiding star, Sir.

With love, Sir,

Ashi Gupta

Senior Creative Strategist, Schbang Delhi

***Comments***

*Bit of introvert and less interactive, Ashi never put herself among front benchers. Perhaps she thought she is not as good as others in the class are. Yet she was a disciplined and sincere girl and was to be watched out.*

*I have always observed that there are some students who undermine themselves, may be because teachers generally leave them unnoticed. I was observing this girl because I knew by nature such students prefer lie low. A year later she started exhibiting her multi-tasking skills & emerged stronger. She moved steadily but towards a definite goal.*

*Pandemic hit hard Ashi. Family suffered because of Covid, and classes went online. I held up this girl in high esteem and boosted her morale. She wanted to pursue PG, but pandemic situation forced her stay indoors. Ashi was reluctant to relocate & she accepted my advice, and went in for a specialized course from MICA, Ahmedabad (online). The skills which she learnt changed her perspective and got an internship with a top brand and today Ashi has embarked upon a successful career in an advertising agency.*

## 'A guide & a friend: Man of varied hues'

*"A person who wouldn't hesitate from calling the shots and simultaneously, would crack me open when needed"*

Coincidence, accident or pure destiny, call it what you wish, but taking up journalism as a career was never in my scheme of things.

It was during the group discussion that I met you for the first time. A senior journalist with a wide range of experience, you had just switched over completely to academics. As my interview round was a complete disaster, I would never want to know what you thought about me.

But my first impression of you was that of a keen observer and a straightforward person with zero tolerance for any nonsense.

While Prof Ratan Mani Lal, a name to reckon with in the field of journalism, showed us the way ahead by sharing experiences and nuggets of wisdom, Johri Sir, you were the one who turned out to be a friend, philosopher and a guide to me.

You would call the shots when situation demanded and would crack jokes to make us students feel comfortable during tense moments.

Personally, I could feel your affection towards me, and the bond only grew stronger with time. You would often heap praise on me for my cartooning skills and it was an assignment for me to draw something daily for the activity board.

The high point was the annual fest where you arranged a dedicated gallery for my works where you enthusiastically guided the visitors.

Towards the end of the course, you were instrumental in arranging for my first job with the 'Northern India Patrika' and again recommended my name for 'The Pioneer'.

Let me take you back to those times in which I got the opportunity to draw for your book 'Out in the Field'; which is nothing short of a badge of honour to me.

It has been two decades of my wonderful association with 'You, Sir' and my love, gratitude and respect for you has only grown over the years.

There can be no better occasion than this to express my gratitude and to thank you for always being there!

With Love, Sir

Avnish Srivastava

Assistant Editor Times of India

***Comment***

*I remember it was in 2002 when I began my second innings as a Teacher with Jaipuria Institute of Management having quit 20 long years with PTI.*

*It was a well thought decision to shift to media academics and share my field experiences with the media students. I was comparatively young loaded with field experience and had a zeal to do something different with young friends!*

*In the second batch of about 75 students, Avnish was different! Bespectacled, Avnish used to be more in thoughts, and his understanding on politics was deep. One day suddenly, I saw some cartoons made in his notebook, and got to know about his love for sketching!*

*We came up with the idea of doing a media gallery! This gallery was unique by the batch of 2002-2003, and Avnish contributed with his interesting sketches & cartoons. I can't remember that such type of gallery would have ever been made than this!*

*Avnish completed his course, and subsequently joined a media house! Calm in nature, Desk was preferred choice for him! And today after 20 years he rose to the rank of Assistant Editor in Times of India.*

*Avnish will always have a special place in my life because the cartoons made by him still attract readers in my first book of journalism, "Out in the Field".*

*My best wishes Avnish. You have miles to go.*

## 'A teacher with a magical problem-solving wand'

*("Believe it or not but you hold a magical wand and can solve anything")*

My story of becoming a tutor in Chicago wasn't at all planned. I still remember my dad asked me and my little sister when I was maybe, in 4th or 5th grade what we wanted to become when we grow up? Without any pause or delay I answered, "I want to be a news reader". My dad maybe wasn't expecting this answer but fortunately didn't show any disapproval.

But this wasn't just a childish dream. This passion to be a journalist kept growing and a day came that after attaining all my degrees I requested my parents if I could join a school of mass communication & journalism.

I saw wonderful journalists and editors as my teachers. I was putting all my heart and soul to soar to the top of this field. The first surprise came when there was a class test and I was absent the day the teacher showed the answer script, however, next day my friends told someone named Abidi has topped in Press laws. And it was me!

Next surprise came up, when you, who was a Senior Editor in PTI (Press Trust of India) gave us a prompt to write. And again, I scored an astonishing remark. I topped in my Journalism School and got many laurels and medals. But that was all, I got selected in Kendriya Vidyalaya and left my job at Hindustan Times and moved to the teaching line since it was a government job that was giving more money and job security etc.

Surprisingly, while coming back to Chicago from Lucknow, on the flight from Lucknow-Delhi, I saw you, and believe me this happened some 15-16 years later from our last meeting…I was in tears.

If you remember, I approached you and asked, “Are you Mr. Sanjay Johri?” And you answered, “Yes!”

It was such a nostalgic and emotional moment for me. Believe me, I am barely making any justice to my expressions here.

Anyway, now I will take you back in time and can certainly vouch on this thought - “Teachers hold a magical wand and can solve anything.”

This happened last year in 2020. My dad who was a strong father and who laid the foundation of confidence and strength in me from a very young age had grown old, he was suffering from dementia, forgetfulness.

With Covid-19 things turned worst, he was made to stay at home, due to Lockdown and his mental anxiety touched its pinnacle and somehow one morning he found way out of the house and was lost.

I was in Chicago, my younger sister was in Bangalore, and my Ammi was alone at home with relatives, neighbours swarming in to help. Unfortunately, they couldn’t do much. I was totally on my prayers and then all of a sudden thought of you, Sir.

No wonder, you being from the media industry helped finding my father, proving me right for what I had been firm on, all my life; “Teachers hold a magical wand and can solve anything.”

This happened in May 2020. Although my dad couldn’t make it for long after that and passed away in August 2020.

Though, he departed soon after his comeback but if it wasn’t you then we would have just lost him in highly dire conditions without having the privilege to bid him last goodbye.

Sir, you definitely must have been a great guide, friend, father-figure, mentor for the rest but for me and my family you have been and are something which we can't express in words.

Thank you, Sir for identifying me and shaping me in the best possible version, and apart from all that for being an utmost saviour for me and my family.

Hope me being in the same profession as yours, someday I get the same privilege to carry your legacy forward.

With Love, Sir

Benazir Abidi

Chicago Public School (USA)

***Comments***

*This is the story of a true relationship between a teacher and student. Yes, Benazir used to be my student in the 1990s, and her writing skills were par excellence.*

*I was new to teaching but had 10 years of experience as field journalist with PTI. While sharing my field experience, I used to put students into reporting, and then would check next day to give my feedback.*

*Benazir was always spot on and stood the best in the class. Subsequently, she went ahead in her journey towards journalism, and then became teacher herself in Chicago after her marriage and settled there.*

*I always remembered her for the talent she had!*

*Years passed and then one day we met in an aircraft and exchanged phone number and email! I While I landed in Delhi, and Benazir set off on a trip to Chicago!*

*A teacher, and a student had to meet again at some point! We had a good old relationship, and I am glad I could do something for Benazir's family!*

*Benazir herself is a teacher, hope she will continue to march towards the heights of success.*

*(This testimonial written by her on Teacher's Day is just in my collections)*

## ‘You believed in me and helped me spread my wings to fly high

*("A mentor, friend and a guide who believed in me, and stretched my potential for good")*

They say some advice can change your life for good. Luckily, I have got tons of them that stayed with me and made me who I am today. This advice can be from anyone, your friend, father, family member, a random folk, or a mentor, LIKE ME. In my journey of being who I am today are the people who are and were there for me when I needed them the most; their wise words stayed with me and will, no matter where I go.

In that absolute gold bundle of people is my mentor, you sir: I am grateful to.

"If you think industry works 9-5, then you're wrong", you said, which is absolutely true, now that I recall sitting in front of my laptop dealing with the hustle and bustle of the industry, reminding me to keep going and more importantly, I CHOSE IT.

A nerd student like me who always wanted to explore and try every possible opportunity in front of her, to her sky was the limit. I never had clarity in my mind about what I really wanted to do in life, which line of work to choose from but you guided me well, and said, "your mind is dicey- bring more clarity in thoughts, talk to people from the industry," but never forced anything on me. He gave me time to decide by myself what I really wanted to do, and look, sir, here I am today doing what you knew I would choose.

Let me walk you back to a memory lane - an incident that changed my life as well.

College life brings you days, both good and bad. Days when you can't help but fall back to existential crises. And supposedly, we don't expect our faculties to understand that, but my mentor did.

There was a day when something major happened in my life that everyone knew about and were looking at me to get the answers, gossips for sure. Somehow, I stretched two lectures of that very long day when I heard that you had called me in your office: I was scared.

But when I entered your office, you rather asked me, "are you alright?" That mere sentence made me cry. I told you everything, you were patient enough to listen to me quietly, and in the end, you assured me not to worry, and it will be fine. Rather you had faith in me and in my truth.

In this world, where people just listen to you for their turn to speak, you spoke to me to listen patiently!

And I think it is that the one thing we all need in life, a person, people, a mentor, to believe in us and show that we all are far more capable than we think.

Thank you, sir, for being that person in my life.

With love, Sir,

Deepti Yadav

Corporate Communication Executive, NTPC

***Comments***

*Unpredictable as one could be at the start of the graduation, Deepti was cool, calm & silent girl but had strong content writing skills.*

*First year is always the time to assess yourself, and a teacher observes a student from a distance. Kanpur girl gradually picked rhythm in the second year and perhaps an internship opportunity made her mature towards roadmap she set for herself. Final year and Covid-19 did impact her plans, but she had decided Public Relations his her forte. She went for a specialized course with Indian Institute of Mass Communication and yes, she bagged a job with top brand MSL.*

*What I liked most about Deepti, she spoke less but whenever interacted spoke about her plans. Self-made girl all set to achieve greater heights and I am sure she has made her plans in the competitive media industry.*

## 'You illuminated my mind in the darkest hour'

*("All things are difficult before they are easy."-Thomas Fuller)*

I am writing to you to say how grateful I am for the mentorship you've given me since 2015. It was winter of 2015 when we first began working together, I never imagined I would be able to make as much progress as I have. Having the opportunity to learn from you has made a substantial change in my life.

I know you're aware of this, but I want to bring this on record, I've always considered you to be just as much of a father figure as you are a mentor. To me, you are always my Popsy!

You not only taught me to take a stand on the right issues but also made me take a back step to get things right. You made me competent enough to take my independent decision and stand by it. You taught me how to face the real world where everything is multi-faceted. You counselled and encouraged me for many years, and I have always known that I could go to you when things seemed darkest.

I don't know how you were always aware of the things which was/is going on in my life, be it professional or personal. I still remember when I got a call from you when I was about to drop from my Ph.D., and when was I was alone in my house sinking in worry and depression. The fact is even today as soon as I call you, you know exactly why I am calling you.

Whenever I wanted to have something let it be food, gifts or even trips it was always a yes from your side. I can't forget all the food you parcelled to me during the pandemic.

I remember how whenever you used to get angry, you would avoid texting back or just a 'hmmm' on call but then also you use to keep an eye on my activities and always made sure that I was on the right track.

The place where I have reached today is because of you, if you would have not given me an opportunity to take classes at Amity, I would never have been in this profession of learning and teaching. I know it's not possible to step in your shoes, but I am sure I will incorporate your teachings in my life and be a person of whom you can be proud.

Thank you for always guiding me back to the right path. I really do not know where I would be without you, other than lost! Your support and teaching have gifted me with perspective and direction.

Last but not least, I want to thank you for understanding and tolerating my coquetry.

With love, Sir,

Dr Kashif Hasan

Head -New Media

MIT International School of Broadcasting and Journalism, Pune

***Comments***

*I don't remember having spotted Kashif a very studious boy when he was doing his bachelor's in journalism in the early years of my joining, and then he moved for his master's from Manipal. We were hardly in touch for about five years, and one fine morning he contacted expressing his desire to be part of our Ph.D. program when we were inducting the first batch.*

*We had no choice since I was the only registered guide, and he joined as first Ph.D. Scholar. The initial years flew by in the framing his research topic for his Ph.D.*

*It was the time, I could watch this boy from Bhagalpur deeper, and he had certain inherent qualities which certainly needed a boost. The tough Ph.D. rules in Amity made him suffer, and he struggled for long. There was a time he went in depression and disgust.*

*I counseled and boosted him up, and since then Kashif never looked back. He completely changed and stood firm irrespective to what may ever come amidst the completion of his Ph.D.*

*During these years, I put him into teaching as a Ph.D. Scholar and what a wonder, he proved as one of the best faculty and darling for students! 500 kms away from parents, the boy faced difficult times during Covid pandemic, and perhaps needed second father in Lucknow. He continued to grow in confidence and emerged victor.*

*Our first full-time Ph.D. Scholar justified his hard work, and Dr. Kashif Hasan was subsequently inducted as Assistant Professor. The foundation was laid, and I knew the boy had to move on from here. He went to become Head of New Media with a prestigious media school in Pune.*

*One of the most loving people with whom I can never forget my association. I can see him occupying the top position in academics.*

*Loads of love & wishes.*

## 'Your support and belief in me are pillars of my strength'

Back in 2020, when I joined the Amity University Lucknow Campus, amongst Covid, to pursue my career in the field of Journalism & Mass Communication, I was kind of uncertain and unsure about myself and the career domain that I have opted for.

It all started, with an orientation programme, in which honestly speaking I wasn't much involved and interactive. Later, when the classes began, I was nominated as the Class Representative of the batch, following which I was motivated and stimulated to work and perform, all thanks to You, Sir.

When I walk down the memory lane, the fondest memory I have, which I am going to cherish for the rest of my life as well was, when you said, 'I see potential and the passion to achieve something, in you'. Being a girl, who always used to doubt and question her capabilities, it was a big cheer up for me.

How I was a mentee of some other faculty, and Sir, you brought me under your Mentee Club, was unequivocally an upliftment in my journey.

Your guidance and support have been the pillar of my strengths, ever since my university life started. You spotted the knack I had for writing and gave me the best of opportunities to come ahead and to prove myself.

There wasn't a single event in which I wasn't a part of, because you believed in me, and knew that I won't let you down. Sir, your affection, mentorship, and attachment for me, became the sole reasons of myself striving hard to thrive and shine.

With successful days, I even witnessed days not so productive. I felt like a loser. And with nobody there for me, it was you, who boosted up my self-confidence and made me believe in myself. I used to and I still irritate and annoy you, constantly with my texts and calls, but there hasn't been a single day, when you have not listened to my cribbing and ranting and had come up with the best solutions for it.

With a smile on your face, you have always provided me with the finest of advice, because you know that 'Confusion and tension is in my DNA'. You know, what's the best for me and from the very beginning, you started to mould and shape me towards the right destination.

Besides, just like a tree protects its branches, Sir, you had protected me too. I would get scolded up for eating cold stuff when my throat is sensitive and vulnerable. I was granted holidays when you knew that I was sick. In fact, you also know my mood and always was aware of the steps I am going to take.

As for my career, and studies, I just can't thank you enough. I am forever indebted to you for your admirable counselling, and for teaching me not only the concepts of journalism but also the concepts of life.

Restricting me from taking the wrong steps when I felt it was right - highlighting my skills and abilities even though people accused him of showing biasness towards me, making me explore my career aspects when I was naïve, acting as a driving force in the enhancement of my personality, comforting and encouraging me on my low days, and most importantly, showering your blessings and best wishes on me, so that I become not only a good professional but a good person too.

If it wasn't for you, I would not have acquired clarity and certitude in my life.

Thank you, sir! Forever grateful to you.

Drishti Vanaik - (Bachelors Final Year)

***Comments***

*Unlucky to start her graduation straight away from online classes belonging to 2020 batch Drishti was the face of the batch along with few other talented students - as I could see her stealing every show and activity.*

*We did not meet for practical classes in the first year, stayed in home amid peak of the pandemic as the first two covid waves consumed the couple of semester examinations. I had her awards and certificates and had to wait to give her in person after first year.*

*The batch returned to campus in physical mode at the third semester and I know had she been physically present in the campus she would have been star attraction in all but maybe we could have witnessed her talent face to face - which she otherwise doing in all the online activities.*

*Drishti not only justified her role as Class Representative, but it was difficult to assume to have an event without her. She proved darling to everyone!*

*One of the biggest aberrations with this girl is her tendency to take too much of tension and pressure and one would find her lost in herself.*

*Despite the fact Drishti is a performer she always doubts her competence and often goes in a shell.*

*Given few unfavorable circumstances, there are times when parents are bound to fall short, and I knew she can be boosted up only by her Mentor. Imagine exams are about to start, and she is the most worried girl. I had mapped her DNA and decided to stay in touch and counsel her during such critical times. She needs to believe in herself but maybe will listen more to her Mentor.*

*What can be more satisfying and proud moment - Drishti has paid nil towards her fees because she has maintained 100 percent scholarship, a rare feat and one among few in the campus.*

*Life is full of struggles and this smart girl is ready to face challenges. Take it from me, she would be a big gun soon in the industry.*

*My love and loads of wishes to her.*

## 'Your pep talks helped me explore my true potential'

*"Somethings can never be repaid; especially in a mentor-mentee relationship"*

As I reflect on back 2018, one of the best decisions that I ever made was pursuing my masters' studies from Amity University, Lucknow Campus and, it was through this opportunity I got the chance to come across you as my mentor.

Although I performed well academically, but there were times when I was feeling uncertain about what I would end up doing with my life? Recalling one such incident, I vividly remember the time when I wanted to take an early joining and was unsure about almost everything in life. I was applying for so many jobs and that came to your notice.

I remember your pep-talks when you used to build my self-confidence by re-affirming my capabilities - advised me to go with the flow and explore my potentials. Although I bagged the first job, a decent one that I applied for, and I was amazed that you were so sure about that fact that I would get it.

Till date I enjoy going ahead with the flow and trusting my journey. Your mentoring enabled me with a greater and different perspective in a lot of ways. It is rightly said that behind every individual there's someone who shaped their life for better. Without your words of wisdom, it wouldn't have been possible for me understand my strengths and the hurdles which I overcame in the process of self-discovery.

Reminiscing the times when you used to pile us up with assignments and deadlines, and you are yet quite stringent with your deadlines! I never had the idea this would help me to understand my shortcomings. I have become way more organized as a person and plan my entire week. This has also helped me a lot in maintaining a healthy work-life balance.

Your support and encouragement have been an asset to my life. I can never repay the time and energy you invested in me by lending an ear to my personal and professional issues. Your valuable guidance has left a deep impact on my life. You believed in my strengths and made me do the same which is why I've been able to turn every hurdle into an opportunity.

Thank you for guiding me with your honest opinions when I was losing hope in me, and when I was unsure of my goals. You understood me and were so thoughtful in showing the right path when I was clueless about where I was heading to!

Please continue showering your blessings on me.

With love, Sir

Fariha Ansari

Market Researcher, VA Group

***Comments***

*The girl from world famous carpet industry town Bhadoi had joined our master's program MA in Advertising & Marketing with a clear mind to learn the nuances and then apply the same in her father's Carpet industry.*

*I was not a regular teaching faculty but as a Director, I interact with students on regular basis and learn about the roadmap for their career. Fariha was thoughtful and determined about her goals. While maintaining high grades, she was part of all the institutional activities and proved her skills.*

*God has gifted me a sixth sense, and I keep spotting students in their day-to-day interaction. There was a time when Fariha would text me and say, 'Sir, can we have an interaction?' And then we would have long session on professional matters, family friends and personal issues, if any.*

*I knew Fariha is all set to embark upon a career she has in mind, and she moved to industry at the right time.*

*I am glad she is going great.*

## 'A guide who motivated me to fight from adversities'

*"A man who has the courage to lead the student for a better future"*

I hope you remember Sir, when I was about to finish my final term, you told me "After 6 months, you would be changed and growing for better future."

You were right. I was changed mentally and physically - overcame my back injury. I have always made you aware of my ups and downs. Of course, we don't talk daily but the conversation has always been a relief.

You motivated me with a sentence *"आप मैं क्षमता है आप लीड कर सकती हो!"* (You are capable and can lead).

Lead was the word that made me release my potential and I started taking up the work and leading that thing. No doubt, since that day, I took the risk to lead and experienced a game changing turn in my life

Today I am working with an international organisation but even leading a team with my new start up – The KIKA Media.

In my farewell speech, I mention you as a father figure, a friend, a mentor and a beautiful human being; that I firmly believe. Courage to lead the student for a better future is his forte, and you never failed.

It rightly said one should always have a mentor in his/ her life who becomes a guiding light when you are in a dilemmatic situation and here, I am 'LUCKY ME.'

You weren't my mentor in the first year of my course, but you failed to guide me in any situation.

Thanks for being there when I needed you the most; in the time when I ruptured my back, and tail bone was impacted.

I always felt embarrassed about using cushion to support my back. The moment you realised about this situation of mine, you soulfully shared your experience with back aches, and encouraged me to step out from the felling of embarrassment and rather embrace the situation.

Since then, I carried that cushion like a side bag which was no more an embarrassment even at the airport, mall or exam hall.

Fortunately, you are a kind of motivator who doesn't just plays around with words rather shares your own personal experiences, high and lows to guide your mentees with better perception towards life and situation dealing tactics.

Thank you again Sir, for such a great gift of perception.

With love, Sir

Kiran Barai

Founder The KIKA (Creative and Media Agency)

***Comments***

*This short-height enthusiastic girl from Mumbai, perhaps the only one from Maharashtra joined us a specialised program 'Masters in Film & TV Production' with a clear focus on learning everything related to production.*

*Fortunately, we had all the facilities & equipment for the students (a batch of just five students), and we gave them all the freedom to lab besides the regular theory.*

*Kudos to Kiran for making best use of this and learn everything she wanted – from ideation to scripting, camera and production. For us she was Miss Dependable. Naughty and over enthusiastic she never missed any deadlines and were part of every production at Amity School of Communication.*

*Having come far away from her home, like every student she too had tough time managing herself at times, but she had good sense of control on emotions whenever she went in crisis. I am happy she shared things with me, and my counselling helped her emerge stronger.*

*She has found her place in the industry and going strong including setting up her own venture.*

## 'Look up to you for solution whenever I am in trouble'

I would be lying if I say that it was just once when I had shared my personal issues with you. From telling you the problems that I was facing in making a right career path for myself, to my health issues to what was happening in my personal inner circle, there have been multiple times when I always seek your guidance.

You have always told me that I am way above these things, and you are extremely proud of what I do. And this sharing of personal experiences did not limit to my college days. It has been almost four years, since I graduated from Amity University, and I still look up to you whenever I have issues. As always, you help me out and tell me these are small things and just are mere parts of life.

I don't think I will ever stop bothering you and reaching out for your guidance.

I recall telling you in your office that this was difficult because it was such a departure from my previous Public Relations and Advertising position. But it was you who proposed that I pursue my postgraduate studies at Azim Premji University.

To be honest, post-graduation was difficult at first, and I recall talking about it to you while walking on the terrace of my dormitory. You informed me how vital it is for me to work hard, stay focused, and not lose my confidence in just one phone call.

One the most important life lesson that I have learned from you is to have a balanced personal and professional life, and nothing should be done heart-heartedly. These words are still on my mind. I only commit to something if I am confident that I will give it my all, and it has aided me in justifying my actions, both personally and professionally, over the years.

I owe it all to you that the past three years have been filled with so much learning!

Sir, look now where I have reached in my life. There hasn't been a time when I haven't told folks that following your guidance has always been the best decision I have ever made.

Thank you for being there always.

With love,

Mahek Nankani

Assistant Program Manager, The Takshashila Institution

***Comments***

*When you move away from home at tender age after secondary education to the precincts of university for higher education sometimes you get excited with the new environment, but it takes time to adjust.*

*This girl from pilgrim city Haridwar was no different as she looked determined to do different in life. Brilliant in academics and equally good in extracurricular activities, Mahek did well throughout but was very confused which industry she should about choosing the right industry for herself.*

*I knew she was meant for Development Communication as career and asked her to focus on institutions like TISS or AJIZ Premji and after a brief stint with industry, she cracked Premji and got out with PG in Development Studies.*

*Sometimes when you are not in parents' company and alone, circumstances distract you and she also suffered from this. She was interacted with me whenever she felt upset, and I am happy to see her bounce back strongly.*

*Miles to go, Mahek!*

## ‘Path shown by you always kept me inspired and grounded’

Since I had come all the way from Jammu to study in Lucknow after completing my Engineering studies, I was always comfortable in the company of senior faculty members. From day one in the class, you always took keen interest in listening to my viewpoints and learning about the events in Jammu and Kashmir. This bonding helped me a lot.

You always guided me and motivated me to think ‘out of the box solutions’ and take initiatives. Under your able guidance we produced PRAYAAS newspaper and ventured out on many local assignments which shaped our careers ahead.

You have always been innovative, sharp and friendly in your classroom teaching, and gave us a platform to perform and we are still learning and trying to come up to your expectations.

I have been working in the field since 2003. During my stay in the campus, you taught us how to survive in this ‘dirty’ world of news making without compromising on your principles. All these years I tried my best to hold on to my ground and never compromised with my work ethics.

All this was made possible due to our grooming in the campus. We were guided by you to do business on your own terms.

You always taught us to enhance our skill set and stay relevant with the changing times. The training and the association of the past two decades is still shaping our career options.

Your teachings and constant guidance always keep me grounded and persistent in my approach towards my life.

With love, Sir

Mohit Kandhari

Special Correspondent,

The Pioneer, Jammu and Kashmir

***Comments***

*I remember the first day of my class with students at Jaipuria Institute of Management when I was taking 'intro' of students - one boy from Jammu & Kashmir said, 'B. Tech'.*

*At a time when simple graduates were opting for courses in journalism, the answer was bit unusual as to why 4-years after his engineering studies this Kashmiri boy wanted to pursue Journalism.*

*Jaipuria had launched a PG Diploma in journalism program in addition to its management courses as they found it market oriented short one year program quite sellable.*

*Fascinated with Mohit Kandhari's answer I called him in my cabin to know more about him. Why are you here all the way from Jammu, I asked, and pat came his reply "Sir, I have always been interested in writing and I think engineering will add value to my career in journalism". Yes, he looked very focused & determined.*

*Mohit proved his determination, and being a field reporter myself, I put him to field assignments. One of the assignments to accompany a foreign journalist to historic city Ayodhya when Lord Krishna birthplace (Ram Janam Bhumi) movement was at its peak, actually brought the best in Mohit, and he grew mature into his reporting qualities.*

*When friends in one of the brand newspapers asked for three interns Mohit was my obvious choice, and subsequently he rose to the rank of special Correspondent to state bureau now in sensitive Jammu & Kashmir - his home state.*

*Keep it up Mohit!*

## 'A perfect blend of mentor, friend & pillar of strength'

A teacher… a colleague… and now a boss!

In the last 20 years, I have seen you in so many roles that it is not easy for me to describe you, Sir.

Sometimes, I praise the 'conscientiousness of the person' who taught you journalism. 5 W's and 1 H runs in your blood. I have seen you as a person who has always been in pursuit of knowledge. The sensitivity of nose for news is same as it was during in your active journalism days.

It has neither withered with profession nor with time. Reporting is no more just a skill for you. It's in your personality trait now. This inquisitiveness in your nature has gradually led to create a counsellor within yourself.

You have not only taught journalism but also life lessons to so many of us. You have seen students growing in their professional career. But in last 20 years, I have seen you growing as an academician and as a mentor.

You have been Bhishma – for all those who needed fatherly advice; Balram – for all those who seek a big brother's assistance; Krishna – for every Arjun who wanted a friendly and ethical lesson of life; and most importantly Hanuman – whenever someone required anyone to take strong stand for them and sail their boat through.

Down the memory lane there are so many incidents in my life where you have played all the above roles at some time or the other. Instead of quoting any particular incident, I would like to draw attention towards your versatile personality, which has been a problem-solver for several students and colleagues.

You first listen to people earnestly, then define their problem and the underlying reasons, generates ideas to overcome, suggests ways to implement those ideas and you keep checking the results from time to time. In true sense, Sir, you are a live example of 'design thinking process'.

Lastly, it is worthy to mention here that despite numerous efforts you put in, you never take credit of the success. In its place, you always acknowledge the person themselves for their achievement. Following couplet *(doha)* stands true on you:

*Guru Gobind dou khade, kaake lagu pai, Balihari guru aapno, Gobind diyo batai...*

With love, Sir,

Mr. Mohit Sharma

Assistant Professor

Amity University, Lucknow Campus

***Comments***

*Born in an ordinary family, Mohit had only come to study the PG Diploma in journalism after his Graduation (Commerce)!*

*He perhaps had no clue what he has towards his career. Always been a back bencher! But he was hardworking! You just put him to a task & he would complete it to the satisfaction of his teachers.*

*After finishing his studies, Mohit got a job in a newspaper and the journey of journalism started. In the initial phase of his life, he faced a lot of struggles!*

*We knew Mohit had a passion and one day he will do something big! After his short stint with newspapers, we brought him into teaching, and he was behind publication of a tabloid for a corporate house.*

*In good old days apart from your education the hard work & experience always paid, and Mohit's success came in handy in 2009 when he started his journey as a faculty at Amity School of Communication, Amity University!*

*I knew that fascination by nature- he liked to walk in the speed of a tortoise but whenever he needed a push or buck up, I tried my best to be his back.*

*Mohit by now had already established himself as disciplined & popular faculty. Hats off to this boy he did his Masters, qualified NET, and soon going to complete his doctorate! I am happy to be part of his successful journey and wish to see him at the top.*

---

## ‘A mentor, a guiding force who groomed my leadership skills’

As my classmates chose me to be the class representative for our batch for the next 2 years (2010-2012 session) I got the privilege to work with closely, Sir.

From any announcements to make to the class to addressing any issue on behalf of the class, you were always present as a guiding force for us. Fortunately, you pushed me harder to strengthen my leadership skills.

From May – June 2011, I did my summer internship under his guidance with Newzstreet India Pvt. Ltd., Noida office. I was constantly in touch with sir, and I used to share my weekly progress report with you.

While writing and publishing my articles at Newzstreet, many times you took personal interest in editing and checking my writing.

I always had keen interest in excelling my writing skills. But you pushed me to work on my communication skills and encouraged me to explore other medium of communication (radio, television as well).

Presently, I work for Tata Consultancy Services Ltd, Bangalore as a senior content writer and I’m also the team leader for the digital marketing project with ten people under my belt.

I am able to make use of the tips and tricks you taught me during my post-graduation days. Most importantly, never to freeze irrespective of the difficult times; moving forward is the key to overcome issues and succeed in career and in life as an individual.

Thank you, Sir for guiding and enabling me with such a perspective of life.

With love, Sir,

Moumita Biswas

Senior Content Writer and Team Leader

Tata Consultancy Services Ltd, Bangalore

***Comments***

*Quieter than her classmates Moumita looked determined to grow, aimed higher in life, and her mantra was 'Content is the King' for all the growth she envisaged during her Masters. Besides the leadership role she was very disciplined and set her goal from the beginning.*

*After her initial struggle while she settled in Bangalore, with TCS, the top consultancy company in India, she still has a desire to pursue her doctorate abroad and has been planning for the right opportunity.*

## 'Your backstage grooming gave us confidence to soar high'

A call from you gives me a fillip as always. But this time it came with a twist. I was apprised that I was chosen to be onboard in your journey as mentor-mentee!

It is not going to be an easy task as there are moments and experiences that can't be put down in words.

The first meeting I recall was in a class of M.Sc. (Tech) in Science and Technology (Lucknow University) way back in 1992-93. The first and the founding batch of its kind and we were lucky enough to get through the entrance.

We got the impression that you are a journalist with a renowned agency and a real master in your profession (we experienced that in the years to come). Your passion for your craft was unfathomable. I remember it was the first of its kind program focusing on Science Communication.

A curriculum focusing on Science & Technology infrastructure, Science Policy & Planning and it centred around how Science Communication can be an effective tool to take Lab to Land program in layman's language. Those were the days when we did not have the modern age technology. The teaching focused on case studies from field reporting, a tool you mastered as a journalist in PTI.

It was your acumen that you worked out a way to get us entry into various functions. Our names were included in the coveted list of Lucknow Media which catapulted us to be a part of all the events in the city including the ones held at Governor House. The point that needs a mention here is that you never took away the limelight and you worked backstage grooming us and giving us the confidence to soar higher and higher.

At one such event the story covered by me got a centre spread with my name… what a moment!

And that too when I was just a student. My professional life never looked back. I got into UNICEF and did a lot of reporting for them. I shifted to Delhi, joined various organizations which included the Indo-German organization where I rose to the position of Deputy Director and travelled far and wide.

The one thing that kept me going was my writing skills which were honed by you. I have been part of newsletters and publications for all the organizations I was involved with till date.

This note would be incomplete if I don't mention the personal influence you had on me. You were not only my teacher-mentor-guru but somehow became an integral part of my personal life. The times spent at your place where we had a small workshop which was a home to a Tabloid Publication - The Other Dimension (I still have all the copies).

Here we got an opportunity to write regularly, and it helped polish our skills. The great journalist minds of Lucknow would edit, teaching us how to write crisp and clear headlines.

Even today when your children achieve professional and personal milestones, I get the emotional connect. My parents have been connected to you even though I left Lucknow 25 year ago.

If I look back more than 30 years back, I think I owe my professional ethics and values to mentors like you. Whatever we have learned gives us the grace and confidence to face the world with our head held high.

May your tribe grow, and more and more students get the privilege to develop such teacher-mentor-guru-friend relationship.

With love, Sir,

Niti Shankar Sharma

Deputy Secretary CBSE (Government of India)

***Comments***

*Contrary to present day about the availability of plethora of courses at different level, professional & specialized courses were not as popular as graduation & PG in Science or humanities led to engineering, medicine, or career in science.*

*DST, Government of India introduced a course MSc- Mass Communication in Science & Technology at Lucknow University to popularize science communication in 90s. Being a Science Journalist with India's premier news agency PTI, Lucknow University requested me to teach students. Niti Shanker was one among the batch of some 15 students.*

*As a young Journalist, I was full of enthusiasm & energy, and if you have good students around your energy gets doubled to deliver. With no-nonsense, we used to have intensive long sessions because the demand of the course was more research oriented, and then dig out science stories for common man. Niti was daughter of a scientist couple and obviously she had a good atmosphere to enhance her knowledge, and plans for her career. Though she was not very clear which industry would suit her.*

*From UNICEF to Indo German organization, Niti did not look back and kept experimenting with her skills to achieve what she aspired to. Relationship with Niti grew between the two families and we cherish our bond with love and respect for each other.*

## 'You discovered my talent and helped me fulfil my dreams'

Sir, I distinctly remember you gave our new class an assignment to write a news story and came to class the next day with all the assignments in your hand. Just one sheet of paper at the top was folded.

That sheet of paper was my assignment and you said it was the only one in the entire class which was very nicely done for a beginner. That is when I realized that maybe I have a talent that was undiscovered by anybody let alone by myself and I should work towards it.

Soon after I was a mentee under his mentorship and you gave me innumerable opportunities and tasks, and it was all mainly focusing on polishing my writing and professional skills.

I was submitting work within deadlines and re-writing and re-doing things unless they were up to the mark. The most important thing you said to me bluntly at one of my articles was 'One can tell it was done in a hurry like you just meant to finish the task and this is not something I expect from Pragya'.

This made me realize that keeping all the procrastinations and college fun aside, I had to focus on my skills, and I can say it surely paid off.

When I was in my last year at Amity, you asked me about my future and put forward an idea to pursue masters in Canada which has been the biggest game changer in my life till now. I was fortunate enough to be his mentee because his daughter had studied in Canada, and it was extremely helpful to have someone at each step of this process to help and guide you.

I came to you with all my queries and confusions, and you never left a stone unturned in making sure I knew what I was doing, to an extent that you made me speak with his daughter over the phone who at that time was in London and gave me her number for any questions.

None of my teachers or any other of my know has been so personally involved in his student's decision, but Sir, you took this in your hands as well and was at my home to make sure my family agrees and gives the green signal.

Nothing in this world can overpower this kind initiative of yours. Hope I live up to your expectations and make you feel proud for this.

I also, wish every student gets a mentor in life like you because that is all one would need sometimes to find their way.

With love, Sir

Pragya Bisen

Franchise Production/ Logistic Coordinator

Brownbag Films (Toronto- Canada)

***Comments***

*I remember during admission of her batch, one of my close friends had called me that his niece is taking admission and please consider her interview. By the time, I could surf through the list a selection panel had already cleared her. Because of her high grades, she was already top scorer.*

*I did observe her but she herself had made a mark with her performance. Fortunately, her batch was perhaps one the brightest one. Pragya was multitasking & I watched her grow as a confident girl. One day during interaction, I suggested her for foreign education, and she had glare in her eyes saying, 'Sir I am also looking at such opportunities.' By the time she completed her graduation she had decided how she is going to persuade her parents to achieve her dream. And she got through in one of the top institutions in Canada.*

*It was her grandfather- a retired IPS and strict disciplinarian who would not allow her granddaughter to go easily, as he wanted to understand the pros & cons of foreign studies. He asked Pragya to interact with me to gain more clarity about it. We had long interaction, and the old man next morning called me to confirm he is depositing fees for Pragya. For me it was mission accomplished!*

*Today the girl from UP's otherwise backward district of Ballia confident is doing great in Canada.*

## 'True to his name, a 'Johri' who discovers, polishes talent'

A small-town boy from Kanpur, I did not know what future had in store for me. Mass communication was a new subject, and I just knew Hindi. The added pressure of not knowing English, it being an intrinsic part of this field, left me quite helpless.

To top it all, being an introvert just added more pressure. As I was meandering through this phase of life that was increasingly becoming more stifling owing to my English language handicap, a gentleman came forward and praised my writing style in Hindi. It was as if a plank was given to a drowning man, which became a turning point for me. I became confident of my abilities and was sure that I was on the right track. Thus, an association began, which has become lifelong.

So, what do I call this incredible man—a teacher, torch- bearer or simply a master craftsman or 'Johri' who spotted a diamond in the muck and has been shaping and polishing it ever since? You must have guessed by now the man that I am talking about. Yes, it's none other than you, Sir.

You honed and polished me for the media world, and I started working with a renowned media house in Lucknow. However, after four years in the same company, I started feeling rusty and the spark, which you had seen in me, started diminishing.

Life had fallen into a rut, and I didn't know what to do, when you once again came to my rescue. You sent me to another media house and here began my real journey into the field of journalism. I learnt to survive and how!

Throughout this incredible journey, Sir, you have been a constant source of motivation who told me to become 'a player made for the long hauls' (*lambi race ka ghoda),* and not a mule succumbing to corporate media world pressure.

It's probably this secret formula that propelled me to challenge myself every day and do something new, which resulted in a lot of creative satisfaction.

Heartfelt thanks to my 'guru' and torch bearer for constant mentoring and motivation.

Thank you very much, Sir for fishing me out on time!

With love, Sir,

Prashant Jha

Brut India Head

New Delhi

***Comments***

*It is a general notion that Bihar produces more bureaucrats, professors & great minds and somehow, I have been highly impressed with the students from this state.*

*Prashant originally from Mithila had joined One Year PG Diploma course at Jaipuria. I spotted this tall cool boy with his beautiful handwriting in Hindi. While our medium of instruction was English, Prashant was always strong in his discussion filled with great general knowledge in Hindi, and I encouraged him.*

*He was very clear and clean in his thought and would love to be part of debates or interactive sessions. Those were great days of journalism where we talked about ethics and morals which unfortunately is missing in present day media.*

*Talented as he graduated, he established himself in media in gradual manner working with Bhaskar Group to Prabhat Khabar but picked up Digital media soon. The best thing about him is he likes experiments and adjust quickly in the situation.*

*It is his experimentation which has taken him to a brand like* **Brut India** *and perhaps from here he is on for a great media journey.*

*I know it is just a beginning for him after having spent 15 long years with the media.*

## "A friendly advice that helped me focus on honing my skills'

If you remember well, Sir, it was you who gave me the first opportunity to anchor for 2018 Amity School of Communication Freshers event that helped me in realizing my skills as an anchor and stage presenter. It was my first time in college when I anchored a program on the stage in front of my professors, seniors, batch mates, and freshers.

With confidence, proper coordination with other anchors, and a bit of sense of humour, I was able to grab and handle the attention of the audience properly and carry that day's event successfully.

It was during my first year when I got an opportunity to share one personal issue with you, Sir. After completing schooling from La Martiniere Boys College, Lucknow, I got selected for graduation in Mass Media at K.C. College, Mumbai. After spending nearly two months there and also performing at St. Xavier's annual fest, I returned to Lucknow as I was unable to settle in Mumbai well.

Post returning, I enrolled in BA (Journalism and Mass communication) at Amity University, Lucknow campus. It was a paradigm shift. For the initial few days, I was unable to cope with the atmosphere here. One day when I decided to share this with you, I felt so relieved and light after sharing my then ongoing issues. You advised me to try to stay unbothered by the external factors and rather focus on the inside; focus more on studies than on the students.

Actually, that advice helped me in focusing on myself and enhancing my skills as a communication student.

You being my mentor once quoted in one of your lectures, "A journalist should have a nose for news, and he should be able to look at the other side of the coin."

I implied this thought process in my work during my internship days with Times of India when they sent me to cover a reality check at Kings George Medical University, for their preparedness against novel coronavirus.

When I visited the hospital, several reporters were there to cover how well equipped KGMU was to handle the outburst of Covid-19 virus. While no one was concerned about the plight of Outpatient Department (OPD) who had come for consultation from neighbouring cities.

They were clueless as the whole administration was busy with the novel coronavirus arrangements. I instantly told this to my superiors, and they asked me to cover that story as well. This reality check story of negligence and absence of doctors and medical staff to attend and guide the general OPD patients got published the next day!

You in fact, instilled the significance of sticking to the deadline in every case. Now when I am in a professional workspace, I realize that day you taught us the importance of disciple and being on time in the workspace. Today, I realize that how important deadlines are and what they can cost you if one tends to ignore them.

Your guidance to act on situations more maturely and deciding by looking at all the aspects, helps me a lot in my decision-making process. During my final year, my peer group was busy enjoying the days while I decided to go for an internship.

They tried to sway me, but your words acted like a reminder. Subsequently, I went for an internship at the Times of India.

It's your inculcated thought process, guidance, teachings and mentoring that helped me in becoming what I am today. I am sure there is a lot ahead of me to learn from you.

Thank you, Sir, for always being there and guiding throughout.

With love, Sir,

Raghav Duggal

PRO UP Environment & Forest Department

***Comments***

*He joined as dashing boy of the batch. We could spot him as decent & disciplined boy in the first year. Though he was multi-talented but was confused about choosing the right industry for himself. I always admired him for his content writing skills and counselled him to go to Advertising or Public Relations. With strong body language and presentation skills Raghav was apt for PR and he landed up as PRO with UP Government.*

*We never knew about his acting, scripting and mimicry. It came as a big surprise when he performed in two big and successful events for his institution at the campus level by organizing students. He is always remembered for raising the institution bar in cultural show.*

*I miss you Raghav and wish a great future!*

## 'You helped me make right decisions, value *sanskars*'

We all will concur that the COVID-19 pandemic had interjected vulnerability into the lives of students, especially pass out looking for jobs. It was time when I was about to complete my last semester and was anxious about placement because hiring was frozen. So, you told me to standby till the time I don't get a company of my choice.

However, that was a bit 'critical' for me to settle with and for obvious reasons. But today I realized, it was the best suggestion and that is because of that, I'm placed with one of the top Public Relation Companies in India. Indeed, patience is a key as fate blesses those who wait.

I can never forget the subject line of your email - "My Long-Awaited Observations." Truly, after reading that mail, I felt like some new energy surged through my veins and reinforced me to its core. The last line of the mail really touched my heart, and that was "Always remember never have Air and forget your Sanskars (Etiquettes). Values always matter in life." Indeed, million-dollar advice.

Every day I follow this philosophy in both my personal and professional life and truly believe that Sanskars and values are the foundation stone of success. After all, in the end, it's not money but, humility and generosity define you.

Whenever I feel like giving up, I simply ask myself "Why have you gone so far when you have to quit in the end? For it is just the place and time that the tide will turn. Hold on! That's my secret mantra.

Once you've determined what you value most and what you want in life, you can turn adversity into prosperity, whether it's about career or personal life decisions. I tell this to everyone - Be Tough, Be Gritty but Never Give Up!

Your guidance, mentoring and understanding attitude towards has always turned out a great combination in setting your students in a right path.

Thank you for being there and guiding me the best.

With love Sir,

Rahul Mohanto

Account Executive

Value360 Communications

***Comments***

*A very enthusiastic from the day one, Rahul ensured his admission in Advertising & Marketing (MAMM) Program as first candidate for his batch even three months before the actual classes began. He was a boy spot on and focused to take up the course with a vision to enter the Public Relations which he eventually did with brand organization - Value 360.*

*Rahul was perhaps the one rare student who not only exceled in his studies but undertook internships one after another during two years of his course which unfortunately, had to be shifted in online mode because of pandemic. Most of his internships were paid and he steadily charted his plans towards the industry.*

*I can see Rahul taking up top position in the industry very soon.*

## 'Your belief in me forced me to push boundaries'

Photography has been my gateway to the multiverse of creative arts that I am part of now. My skills as a photographer improved manifold during my time at Amity University and the credit goes to my mentor, you, Sir.

There are several times when we mentally require an assurance to move forward into the many avenues of life. It was your belief in me as a creative artist that made me discover the inner photographer in me.

Towards the end of my bachelor's degree in 2016, you encouraged me to participate in a poetry recital. I was hesitant, but you gave me the extra push I required, and I found my love for poetry.

You never stopped believing in me. Trusted my abilities and during my final year project, gave me an opportunity to work with Oxfam India, and lead a team to cover a series of photographs for their campaign called 'Aroh'.

We had to cover the lives of women farmers in Uttar Pradesh. In retrospect, which would be one of the times when I felt that my dedication towards the project had increased. Your trust in me enabled me to manage the campaign and also gave me an opportunity to setup and host an exhibition in an annual event in University Campus.

In 2015, I met with a terrible accident and could not attend college for a few months, you then stood by me and ensured that when I was ready to resume. I would not find it hard to catch up with everything that had happened in class. You had put in extra time and effort to ensure that I stay up to date on every lesson.

For that, I am eternally grateful to you. I have never forgotten everything that you had taught me. We've known each other for years and I never miss an opportunity to see you whenever, I am in town.

I am always certain that in each meeting, I would be encouraged to move forward towards my dreams more than my ambitions. It is important to understand the sense of freedom - for creativity to be achieved, thus my years at Amity University with you will remain a landmark in my ongoing journey ahead into this field.

With love, Sir,

Razi Ul Hasnain

Independent Photographer & Entrepreneur

***Comments***

*Razi in the first year of his graduation was bit of shy or someone whose talent was hidden. One would find him absent in the morning classes because perhaps he was late riser. Since, I used to teach first years for Print Journalism, and kept an eye on such students. I had to call him and find out what is wrong with him? In fact, while interacting with him, I learnt about his interest in photography. I got a clear picture about a career roadmap when he shared his photography work with me. The best thing for such students is to put them to a task which interests them the most.*

*Razi literally constituted institutes 'Photography- Club' and was instrumental in organizing an exhibition on Photography. He took charge of the event and brought laurels to the institute! Having a background of La Mariniere Boys, he was par excellent in his oratory skills.*

*An accident, and subsequent long recovery brought him closer to me and his family because he needed support and morale boosting from someone. He bounced back even stronger and then there was no going turning back for this boy.*

*Razi went to Jamia for his PG Course and then to UK for highest studies. Today, he has a successful career.*

## 'You nurtured me like a child to bring out the best in me'

Like a father, who wants nothing but the best for his children, you always caught me off guard. This was one of the many instances which reflected that you knew me better than I knew myself.

You always managed to take the length of hours to guide your mentees when HODs are commonly perceived to be typical, unapproachable, and conservative; with you I could discuss about anything - world affairs, life and personal well-being, college, faculties, and students.

Literally anything which you deem is important for the betterment of your students.

Initially, I was hesitant to bother you with my things, but you persuaded me to engage in having open discussion with you about everything. I remember visiting your cabin with my medical reports for jaundice. After having a look at it you advised me to go back to home, long away to Indore, and advised me to take care of my health solely and keep the rest aside.

From our first interaction you made out that not only would I make it through the admission list of the college, but also to the list of your mentees. You had seen something in me, encouraged and kept on giving me multiple chances.

I was naive and childish to have entered and graduated from college. But you kept me listed on every possible project, which helped me to gain industry-based experience, right from my teenage years. I keep a dear record of them in my CV, and that has worked out well in my CV throughout!

I am filled with great regards and admiration for the role Johri sir has played in my life. He has nurtured me to become better at my shortcomings to thrive happily.

Your wisdom and support had worked out to bring a better in me. I know not, however, if I have been kind enough to his goodness. But I certainly will keep striving to exceed his expectations and hold on to your good books.

With love, Sir

Ridam Khare

SEO & Content Specialist

Expand My Business

***Comments***

*Always inquisitive, I will remember Ridam for being ready with a question whenever I conducted Print Class. He was updated on current affairs and would not even hesitate to argue sometimes to my anguish. He was logical, was loved by one, and all among his faculty. If there is a debate competition in the university or outside, he would be a nominee. Strong with content Ridam developed himself in scripting as well as anchoring later.*

*I still remember him as one who suddenly got distracted and even started avoiding me. Being his mentor, I used my network to find out what was going wrong with this talented boy. And, when I got hold of him, he admitted his distraction to 'wrong company.' It's better late than never and Ridam came back to his usual rhythm! You have a great future ahead Ridam.*

## 'You inspired me to work without fear or favour'

Teachers play an essential and vital role in everyone's life. Some of them are "Johri". It is difficult to explain in words that how and to what extent had you been able to guide me in my career.

I remember, you always taught us every lesson of journalism with your personal experiences as a reporter. It means a lot for me always, Sir. Twenty years have passed, but I still remember each lesson.

You used to tell us that how a chief minister tried to influence you in his helicopter and offered you a residential flat in Lucknow, so that you would send a favourable report to PTI headquarter about his election rallies. But you never did so! In early days of my career as a reporter and bureau chief of a regional news channel, many times I got such offers, but I always remembered your lessons.

In my career as a reporter, I never filed a false story, I never provoked any person or group, so that I could get a breaking news. Behind me this approach, I find you, Sir. Once, you told us in classroom that how a superstar reporter of electronic media provoked "shivsainiks" on valentine's day to attack on an Archies showroom in Kanpur and telecasted exclusive video on his news channel. You taught us that it is not journalism. I remember it, as of now.

The first quality of a journalist is 'nose for news'. I believe, I have it. I think, I found this sense because of your teachings. Your guidance still affects my perception style. You know your students better than they do about themselves.

I recall, it was the first week of mass communication's first batch's orientation in Jaipuria Institute of Management. We all met up in college campus to celebrate republic day. Suddenly, the management asked you to send a mass communication student to deliver a speech on the occasion. You just asked me to do so in a hurry. All eyes were on me. I was not prepared for such moment. But I spoke up with confidence and everyone praised my speech, which I delivered randomly without preparation.

I don't know, why did you believe in me. How did you figure out that I could do the job? You are always aware about your student's potential. I have much more to say, but the word limit won't allow me for it. I would like to end it here by thanking you, Sir, for your contribution in my career.

With love, sir

Rishi Kant Singh

Senior Editor,

India TV

***Comments***

*First and founding batch we launched at Jaipuria Institute of Management for one year PG Diploma in Mass Communication & Journalism - we did not know about the response.*

*It was huge and we got mixed bag of students from Bihar to Jammu & Kashmir, in addition to Lucknow. This was perhaps the first institute of its kind in north India which was headed by eminent journalist like Mr. Ratan Mani Lal and a few hardcore media professionals like me from Press Trust of India.*

*We had some ambitious plans to deliver and train students industry ready from day 1. Rishi Kant Singh from Sasaram*

*Bihar was typically Bihari with inquisitive mind and in my dossier of each students' files, I could see the talent in him.*

*Well-read Rishi Kant was spotted as most curious one in the class, and a person with curiosity. We did not go for a very structured timetable as we allowed classes to go on for longer duration if students wanted extended interaction.*

*Even if the classes got over by 4.30 pm, I sat with students for long over a cup of tea at Ramesh Chacha's (uncle) hamlet - giving it a place to discuss & debate! We as a journalist are trained with ethics and rules of journalism, and we wanted these cub reporters to emulate ourselves.*

*Rishi showed his spark during the extra-curricular activities, and he was a great debater. What can be the satisfaction for a teacher if he finds his Mentee following the same ethics and values today that we preached. Today he is a Senior Editor in India's prominent news channel.*

*I know Rishi has never compromised himself in a time when Indian media is hardly able to deliver.*

*Thanks Rishi you have made a mark and made us proud!*

## 'Your professional mantra showed me the path to grow as a scribe'

What a spectacle!

A greenhorn journalism student assiduously sitting on her lecture chair waiting for the teacher (An expert from 'the industry' with an exhaustive reporting experience, as was explained by another lecturer), it was quite an interesting experience to see a man with horn-rimmed spectacle walking slowly along the seated row of students with a pen clipped in his front pocket, newspaper and attendance register in hand.

After meticulously putting the newspaper and attendance register on the desk, Sir, you introduced yourself in a matter-of-fact style and thus began an association with a teacher, that finally culminated in a boss, colleague and lifelong mentor-mentee bonding apart from a similar career trajectory from journalism to an academician.

The 18 odd years that have elapsed since my first meeting with you, one thing that impacted me the most was his attention to details and the importance of being good at paperwork. In journalistic parlance it literally translated into recording and keeping all the information while reporting, editing as you never know when it might come in handy.

This not only helped when I joined the Times of India as a reporter in 2003 and covered various beats including politics but also in Delhi when I started working with a business magazine as a special correspondent in 2005 and later in the Hindustan Times (HT) in 2007 were joined on the desk as a sub-editor.

Your professional mantra on punctuality, sanctity of meeting deadlines and confirming veracity of news/information helped me a lot as I became the junior-most person (sub-editor) in the Lucknow edition of the Hindustan Times to head a team that launched its two prime editions- Dehradun and West UP.

Later, I started heading various desks including Eastern UP edition, Varanasi and Prayagraj editions. Gradually seeing my diligence and knack for politics, which I had covered earlier, I was made part of the election desk in HT, which was a big learning experience.

Finally, after 15 years of active journalism, I felt the urge to share my experiences with youngsters and thus began my foray into academics where once again I encountered you as Head of Institute (HoI) ASCO, Amity University. After a detailed discussion with you, I joined ASCO as a faculty teaching print media in 2019.

Three years have flown by and now working with the man who still sports horn-rimmed spectacle with a pen clipped in his pocket and the newspaper now replaced by phone, the journey with my mentor has been a noteworthy spectacle!

Thank you, Sir, for nurturing me for what I am today.

With love, Sir,

Sangeeta Pandey

Consultant Ogilvy

***Comments***

*A well-read girl would always sit in the front row of the bench on the left side of my class. Perhaps she wanted to sit in front and tell that she was brilliant or wanted to listen and observes teachers closely!*

*Sangeeta was a student, and she not only proved this by doing her course successfully, but also walked with determination on the same path as to make a career! Sangeeta was my student in the 90's, and we were not in touch for a long time.*

*But you do not forget the meritorious student!*

*Suddenly one day his phone rang, and we brought back our old memory. Sangeeta now had 17 years of media experience and wanted to become a teacher!*

*As a collaborator, the pair of Mary and Sangeeta got involved in teaching print media - as we both shared our field experiences with the children, and also prepared them for their professional journey!*

*The loudest was when some of the media shared their joys, and sorrows during their leisure time. Along with the media industry, Sangeeta has now also mastered academics.*

*I believe she'll go further with this.*

## 'A go-to-friend, a guide & a loving guardian'

As we move past different stages of our lives, we meet many people and bond with them on different levels. Some become colleagues, some become friends, or even extended family. However, there is another relationship that you might not actively be searching for, but when you have it with someone, you know how much you needed it in your life. It is between mentor and mentee, a relationship that blurs the line between a guide and a friend.

When I first joined Amity University Lucknow in 2019, I had made a rather huge and controversial transition from the field of Medicine to Communication. I was constantly dealing with self-doubt that was detrimental for the beginning of a new chapter in my life. However, my first encounter with Prof. Dr. Johri sir pulled me out of this constant spiralling. In his first lecture he asked all the students to write why they joined the institution. Overwhelmed as I was, I poured all my thoughts and ended up handing out three pages for a small class activity which I thought would go unnoticed. Unexpectedly, he not only took my papers home but read them and got back with his remarks on my write-up later and this is how I met my mentor.

That gesture was just the beginning of a relationship that assured smooth-sailing rest of the way. From taking out time to offer undivided attention whenever I needed to share about any and everything hampering my personal and professional growth, health issues, to financial issues, family issues- you name it; he helped me get through the many rough patches of life and come out stronger. Striking the balance between friendliness, leniency and much needed strictness when it came to discipline, Johri sir made me a more sorted and self-directed adult who finally feels like she is in the driving seat of her life now.

While you cannot measure something so pure with numbers, I scored a rather average 8.05 SGPA in the first semester of my college and by the end of graduation I have topped with 9.29 CGPA, bagged a job at one of the most renowned Indian media outlets- Aaj-Tak, and get closer to becoming a well-rounded individual. While I still have a long way to go, I owe the tiny landmarks in my life to my mentor who aced the roles of a go-to friend, a guardian, and a teacher- all at the same time; for which no amount of "Guru Dakshina" can ever repay.

Sanjana Saxena

India Today

***Comments***

*Commencing her graduation in 2019 in regular face to face mode Sanjana had shown her spark from day-1 with her excellence in academics, regular participation in extracurricular activities including some scintillating dance performance and won several prizes for that too.*

*We had every reason to believe she is a new find of her batch. She is a great learner, and it was this skill which made her entry into the University Digital Club (UDC) - as a key member which she continued for more than two years during her graduation.*

*Covid-19 impacted heavily as the batch had to shift to online education, something which deprived her from showing his talent. Hats off to Sanjana despite all odds she faced the situation bravely ensuring whatever she missed, she covers the moment, and we returned to physical mode. Such students are rare who fight back and then top the course winning maximum awards.*

*Her contribution with Institutes partnership with UNICEF will go down in the annals of ASCO history because she was not only a key performer but conducted live sessions too.*

*I knew Sanjana's talent and when India Today came up with just one vacancy, she outscored leaving behind three others and today holds a key position with India's top brand and performing multi-tasking roles. This is just a beginning for this short height girl who is capable of breaking shackles to prove her point.*

*Miles to go Sanjana Baby!*

## 'As a mentor, you tamed the chaos within me"

Initially I aspired to be a doctor, but with abundance of talent in the same field I failed, and I am glad I did so because if I hadn't failed, I wouldn't have gotten the chance to meet **My Tamer**, well yeah that's exactly what you did to me, you tamed me from a wild bull to a calm cow.

When I had given up hopes from all the other places that I once aspired to be a part of, I entered the doors of Amity and met you; the HOI of the ASCO Department because all I wanted was to be counselled, as to what to do, where to go. I still remember your words when you first met me, "I see the spark in you". Well, that's exactly what enlightened the spark within me.

Everything that I could achieve was only because of you Sir. The way you calmed my chaos and the way you supported me; it definitely helped me grow as an individual. I remember how before every exam I'd come up to you for your blessings and get angry when you forgot to give them to me.

Well, this is exactly how our relationship wasn't just of a mentor and mentee, it was more of a father and daughter. On my darkest days you showed me light and cheered me up when I had nobody by my side. I often did lose hopes easily, but it was your motivation and guidance that kept me going through the storms of life.

Today I can't be any prouder to say this, but you have been my Godfather since day one and all that I am today is the result of your patience and efforts. I wouldn't have achieved anything without you, Sir.

From my success to my failures, you have seen it all. I am grateful forever.

With Love, Sir,

Saumya Singh, Deputy Manager HRBP, Axis Bank

***Comments***

*One of the most difficult girls I have come across during my stint in academics. A super intelligent Soumya did not know what she wanted to study after her intermediate. She cleared medical entrance and then did a course in Interior Designing but left both.*

*Looking for some other options, she landed in my institution to try if Journalism can be an option for her. All through the discussion, I understood her confusion, frustration and perhaps she needed patient hearing. I quietly listened and gave her a piece of paper to write 300 words on any topic she liked. She returned with an amazing content. Obviously, School of Communication was the right place for her.*

*As she entered the second year, Saumya made her plans clear to pursue MBA and joined the coaching. She cracked top IIM institutions, but Covid conditions forced her to move to Nirma Institute (Gujrat) and got placed with a good package.*

*The difficult girl, as I said literally made my life hell because at every step when she had some problem, she would be outside my cabin, and sought to interact & share her issues. And the best thing was that she always followed the advice.*

*I had to even put an alarm in my clock to wish her in the morning before her exams. In case, if I forgot, she would text me 'Sir wishes needed.' She graduated with university's top honours.*

*Cheers Saumya! You will achieve what you have dreamt about yourself.*

## "You taught me to introspect, be responsible, forgive & forget'

School and college life, perhaps, are the most enriching and memorable times of an individual's life. My high school experience allowed me to exhibit my skills as a National Debater and Declaimer and I won accolades to my name.

I was driven toward Journalism and Mass Communication. Since then, I have wanted to explore the basics of marketing, communications, journalism, and entertainment. My camaraderie with oration, creative writing, and communication made me feel worthy of becoming an aspiring communication student. When I entered the portals of Amity School of Communication (ASCO), I had no idea that twelve years later, teachings from the you 'S M J' rulebook would be so valuable to hone my skills and capabilities.

During my first year at ASCO, the department hosted its annual event, Via Media, for its students to showcase their skills, a chance to innovate, a chance to show their creativity, and a chance to discover themselves as individuals, going far beyond the confines of academics.

The orator and content curator in me could not stop participating, so I showcased my skills. That was when I got a chance to meet you, the Director of Amity School of Communication. You cherished my content curation and oration and became my mentor for life. Sir, you helped to make me profound, potent, and independent.

I clearly remember an incident when as an immature college girl, I made a few mistakes and didn't know what to do then you guided me well. You told me that we tend to make mistakes, how we then look without observing, how we listen without understanding, and how we trust without knowing.

We, as human beings, have designed with flaws. Our eyes trick us, our stories change in reiterating, and how life sets us up for irresistible blunders. Although teachers tend to educate us that making mistakes will not lead us to success, ironically, you taught me that if we make mistakes, we are human. You taught me the ability to introspect, take responsibility and apologize, cut some slack, and learn to forgive and forget.

Your mentorship has played a significant role in my career development. I am working as a Marketing and Communications Manager at Rakuten Symphony, one of the largest telecom giants across the globe, making significant strides to accomplish the goals set by the company.

When I was graduating, I knew I was a content curator and a communicator. My ability to concoct stories, write creative content, and communicate through it never let me switch to any other career. Even today, I make mistakes because I am human, but I introspect, and if I can correct those mistakes, I don't wish to build the walls of not learning from making slipups.

Sir, you were one of my best critics; I never really witnessed your appreciation or applauding for me; you always expected more. This, perhaps, made me go the extra mile. Your guidance and mentorship have immeasurably helped me in my personal and professional life.

Sir, I cannot thank you enough for this kinship, guidance, and encouragement.

"Your influence on my life extends beyond Amity, well into the future, into my life."

With Love, Sir

Smriti Sharma D.

Marketing and Communications Manager

Rakuten Symphony

***Comments***

*She looked very calm by nature and even remained unnoticed for me when I taught her in the bachelors first year. Maybe some students don't like to show-up but want to be noticed by their talent which happened with Smriti.*

*I recognized her talent in the second semester from when Smriti started exhibiting her multi-tasking abilities! She has amazing writing skills!*

*Extremely disciplined, one who took initiatives, and you give a task to her - Smriti won't sleep till she completes even if she had to work till 2 late in the night! I generally share SMJ Rule book with all my mentee. Luckily, Smriti had understood it perfect because she knew how to keep me happy.*

*Smriti as she moved into senior semesters grew mature and came up to our expectations in whatever role given to her. She was part of the Team Trusted!*

*Yes, there came a time when she was completely distracted and had to face my wrath too. She certainly got a lesson to come back strongly & since then did not look back!*

*Like any Web Series an artist in the next season appears stronger in the characterization and it seems like in Smriti Season-2, she is in a new avatar. I consider her a strong woman with substance, dedication, and discipline both as a Senior Manager and managing family very well.*

*In five years from now I can see her as CEO of a brand company.*

*Loads of Love & wishes Smriti*

## 'Your support made me feel secure and confident'

Like every third person, I also faced a lot of struggles as soon as I entered college.

It was very difficult for me to handle multiple issues with boys from different departments. I still remember the time when I shared this thing with my you and fortunately, you were no less than a concrete wall that guarded me throughout.

You didn't just take very serious action against people involved in the matter but also informed about the same to their respective HODs. After that, I felt so secure, so confident to face such people because I knew that there is someone who is there to help me out in every situation possible.

Though there is a lot of guidance by you that is worth applying to - one of the most important qualities that I always look up is the way you handle your department with such calmness and efficiency.

I have always been a very short-tempered girl and to impart training to people who are double my age was no less than a task. I always look up to you Sir and try to acquire your calmness in the workspace.

Straight after completing my masters, I was offered a job in a PR agency where they were asking me to get into a contract with them and also wanted me to travel.

Since the job package was quite attractive but I didn't want to make any wrong choice with my first job, so I consulted with you right away. You shared the insights of the industry and what exactly the company was expecting from me. Such guidance was no less than a boon to me.

It gave me a crystal-clear picture in terms of my job profile and industry working atmosphere.

Thank you, Sir, for being there as my safety net at my lowest and for your guidance through-out.

With love, Sir

Sneha Nanda Negi

Hishu Solutions. Manager- HR and Training.

***Comments***

*Very few students show dedication and discipline to their studies, and career from the word go. In fact, Sneha was a No-Nonsense girl when I interacted with her in the initial days. Studious as she was, she never compromised with the indiscipline of fellow students. I remember her when she came with a complaint as to why students in the University Canteen look differently when they see a girl. Why can't they grow mature? She was furious and had to be counselled.*

*For me it was her discipline and leadership quality which persuaded me give her some big responsibilities on a partnership we had with an Australian Company. The reputation and outcome of the project we had was all because of Sneha.*

*Today she leads HR in a reputed company, and I am told she is indispensable for the Directors.*

## 'You taught me how to always be there for others'

Who has had the most influence on my life? I eventually received my answer after thinking about it for quite some time. My professors. Since I was a child, I've never considered what I wanted to be when I grew up.

Everyone else was setting goals, but I was just enjoying the process of learning; the classroom atmosphere was usually exciting. Learning was a really rewarding experience in and of itself. I believe I can say this since I encountered teachers who were enthusiastic about their work at various levels of my education.

I enrolled in a bachelor's course in journalism and mass communication in the hopes of learning more about the people skills and qualities, I assumed I possessed in order to work in the media. During the first year of the course, I was looking for my calling but couldn't seem to discover it.

Our true skill, it is believed, lies in the things we become unconsciously adept at. Being taught by you as the department's head was impressive enough, but it was an extraordinary thing for me - having you call me up and tell that I am good at something.

When you saw that I have an aptitude for writing, I was completely oblivious of it. You had seen me take the stage and finish the job every time.

As my mentor throughout college and my work, you have been a blessing in disguise. Because you spotted potential in me, my ambition of working in a university became a reality.

You never left any stone unturned in ensuring that all of your students receive the opportunity they deserve. Having someone in a life who can be an educator, mentor, and lends his ear on occasion makes this journey much more enjoyable.

You have had such an impact on so many students because you are so invested.

Sir, you have made an indelible imprint on so many of us during your tenure. Thank you for teaching us how to be there for others.

With love, Sir

Sonia Singh

Content and Brand Manager, Amity University

***Comments***

*It is not necessary that you spot talent in a student from the day one, and same was the case with Sonia who joined the Graduation Course like many other students.*

*She however looked someone to be watched out. Her content was strong, and she was a straightforward Punjabi girl (Kudi).*

*She took time to understand the atmosphere, and the course. I spot seriousness in her in the second year. She was intelligent, and proved it with her high-grade during graduation, but she took time to plan her road map.*

*After a short stint with the industry, she decided to go for post-graduation. She however could not adjust in hostel life may be because of home sickness.*

*After taking a break, Sonia then joined back for her masters with us, and this was the turning point for the girl. Like took a turn and she was transformed with high energy, and front runner for University's top honours which she eventually got!*

*Sonia was now mature and brimming with confidence! She gained experience with an industry job, and then rose to the heights of success.*

## 'You inspire me to move ahead, decide and act'

Sir, you were the one who believed in me during campus placements in 2011 during my UG final semester and inspired me for the interview rounds, through which I got the opportunity for campus placement and attended an international event 'Arab Health' on behalf of the firm in Dubai, UAE.

This is not the only instance, but you have always inspired all the students and colleagues to move forward, make decisions, and act accordingly. You have been a leader who takes responsibility for those who work under you and always support them in all thick and thin. Under your leadership everyone gets the opportunity to grow. You always promoted the work of your students and subordinates always given credit for the work.

Your consistent support, trust, and direction have helped me through both professional and personal ups and downs over the last 14 years. You pushed me work so hard that my efforts were acknowledged both on campus and at the head office level.

You have always created a congenial environment for effective in-house training, instilling confidence, and bringing out the best in people. Thank you for motivating me to think critically and work harder.

Thank you for teaching me how to read between the lines. Your practical teachings and day today inputs have taught me more than what I've learnt from any book or a website. I attribute my present professional success to the team management ideas you've shared with me.

You have always been 'understanding' to any personal or professional concerns that have been discussed with you through a process of first 'listening' and then offering your 'life mantras' based on your experiences - which have always worked as a great solution to the situation.

You are an inspiration, a person who, despite your numerous health challenges throughout the years, has always pushed for exceptional outcomes. I know you since 2009 and it's truly a wonderful experience to know you as a Teacher, Mentor, Guide, and as a boss…

Thank you so much for all that you have done for me.

You have worked tirelessly to help me in any way you saw possible. The vital skills I've learned from you will stay with me as I continue to develop professionally and personally.

With love, Sir

Soumen Bhattacharya

Manager- Digital Media & Communication

Amity University (Lucknow Campus)

***Comments***

*He looked like a cute guy (babua) in the class! An unassuming boy who was nothing more than ordinary! One could not guess anything about his talent!*

*With elderly mother, and the only child in the house, sometimes he looked more mature than his age. Actually, his priority was to stay with his mother as he knew about his responsibility.*

*His strength was his confidence! Radio was his forte, and he set out to make a career in the FM channel! He also did an international tour, and from here he gained in his confidence. Since post-graduation is always necessary to enhance your knowledge, he preferred MBA in Media Management.*

*This is where his success started and made him earn a place in the industry. Being emotional is his biggest weakness, and even today he needs my advice because he believes my one dose works like adrenaline.*

*Babu Moshai has a great future ahead and all set to earn his doctorate too.*

## 'No better experience than staying in your company'

A hard-core field Journalist and Reporter with Press Trust of India, Sanjay Mohan Johri was not only just a teacher but a true guide for me whose teaching was not only confined to Classroom but more as a Life Coach.

Down memory lane, I still remember when you taught 'Reporting' as a Guest Faculty at LBS in 1993, and shared your previous day field assignment – especially, the stories you had planned to do. Besides the basic rule of 5 W's and 1 H, you shared your own experience and then explained your approach to the class.

You always believed the 'Classroom learning' has to be complimented with 'Experiential learning' because in future students would be required to face similar situation in the industry. Your tips are still of great values and irrespective of my position today, I don't just use these tips for myself but also guide my team to follow.

I have no hesitation in admitting that I was one student in the front row ready with long list of questions and Sir, you would sit beyond the class hours to answer all such questions. You gave us regular field assignments and would check next day suggesting corrections with your 'red' pen. There were no computers, Google *Baba* in those good old days.

I remember some of your classical stories (scoop in media terminology) when you shared how a small tip which you got in a research lab became a big headline in national stories; after you investigated them for days after travelling from one place to another. You had many such stories to your credit.

One doesn't need someone to guide just in the classroom, but one also needs a Mentor who can help us through our professional journey. I built a strong relationship both personal and professional and I cannot forget the day when I informed you about my selection in a brand newspaper.

"This is just a beginning! Take it from me, you will be the youngest Editor of a newspaper one day", pat came your Ashirwad. What I am today is because of Gurus' blessings. All your predictions about me proved correct. Perhaps you believed in me from day one.

While you had quit active journalism in 2002 to move to media academics, but my association continued and there were occasions when we debated, argued but this only strengthened our bond.

I remember when I was offered first international Fellowship, I needed help from someone to write the proposal and who could have been better person than you, Sir.

Impressed with my growth in the media you always wanted me to come and share experiences with students at your media school and it was dream come true when I shared stage with you on several occasions.

You always took pride in sharing with the audience about my struggles and then traveling this path. Sir, you showed your nobility to share many platforms with me and always gave respect though I felt nervous at times on such occasions.

The knowledge of a 'Guru' is always immense and meaningful.

It is my endeavour to pass on whatever I learned, from my all Gurus to the next generation, and benefit them for their learnings.

There can be no better experience & satisfaction than staying in the company of such a simple and honest journalist of 1980s, the time when the media days were different.

I am happy to be your student of that era.

With love Sir,

Sudhir Mishra Editor

Navbharat Times New Delhi

***Comments***

*Coming from a middle-class family with limited income, Sudhir had a determination to do something different in life.*

*I remember him as someone as very disciplined and sincere boy in the class who was always in time, and would like to stay beyond class timing since he had loads of question bothering him – about how a journalist can bring change in the society?*

*He was always interested in long conversations with the teacher even after the class was over! Often, we would find him coming to our media offices if he had a query.*

*I consider Sudhir as one of the rare breeds who started his journalist journey in an evening newspaper without any honorarium as soon as he finished the course. He worked for quite a few years on a paltry salary but for him running around the day and chase a story irrespective of it being a big or small. The satisfaction for being is the process of it had always been primarily achievement for him.*

*One could spot him at every happening place. Sudhir was not only a correspondent for his newspaper but a Khabri (person with nose for news) for we all journalists since many of us miss covering all the happenings in the city.*

*A never-ending appetite for news, writing features and reaching a troubled spot were some of the qualities which helped him progress from one media house to another brand with today heading one of the most popular, Times group in India.*

*I always had only one prediction for him - to be the youngest editor of a newspaper! And he achieved.*

*His journey in media continues but you never know about Sudhir. He is always filled with so many ideas that one day you may find him exploring an unexplored area. He always tries to fight with the system but with honesty in his writings. He is never afraid of taking risks!*

*As a teacher & journalist, I am always proud of him. We continue to argue and debate & its unique about our relationship & keeps our bonding strong!*

*Wishing him many more long years of accomplishment.*

## 'Your guidance always yields positive results in work and life'

I've had some reservations initially when I went up to the stage. But I have to tell you now, I eavesdropped (not intentionally) when you were talking to a faculty member about an event. While the said professor was not sure if I should be the one addressing everyone at the event, you were confident I can do it. "I think you have missed it. Trust me and let her go up on the stage," you said. It was just the beginning of my term and that "trust" made sure I gave my 100% to not let you down throughout my graduation.

I have had a lot of instances when I shared my personal issues/experience with you. I have well tried, tested, and firmly believe, 'Understanding' is the word that defines solutions to all my problems whenever I shared something with you.

The credit of me stepping into the professional arena goes to you single-handedly. Right after my graduation, when my parents and I were unsure if I should move to a new city, you invited us to your house, introduced us to your family and your loving dog and showed me how it would be the right thing to do. I'm glad you took that extra mile and now four years later, everything you said would happen, is happening.

There have been instances when you have been highly critical to my work. There was a Science Film Festival, you asked me to conduct the session and I missed a few points. Without blinking an eye, you told me I lacked in my research and how ordinary craft is not acceptable in the industry. It is still encrypted in my brain and it's a daily reminder to be thorough with my stories.

Though there are many which I imply sub-consciously in my working style but one utmost thing that you said was "Don't make decisions when you're overwhelmed." You told me when I was picked in one of the competitions and I was ready to give up my classes in the first semester itself. It has stayed with me. Whenever I'm to decide on something, I make sure I'm not 'overwhelmed'.

The implication of your guidance and words never fail to yield positive result in my work and life decision making skills.

Thank you very much for being my mentor for life, I am yet to achieve something and make you proud.

With love, Sir,

Vaishali Jain

Sr. Sub Editor India TV

***Comments***

*Unassuming but Vaishali was a girl with a difference who was watched by me for her multi-tasking talent. Though reluctant about herself, yet she had the guts to perform whatever task I assigned - in-house research or performance on stage. She was the choice of one & all because she had the discipline.*

*I remember when one of my media friends, and Sr. Editor asked for recommendation for someone multi-tasking, Vaishali was the right choice and later she became indispensable for the organization. Even the Editor friend did not stop her when she decided to move on and switch to other bigger brand because this little-tiny girl had to spread her wings in the industry.*

*That level of talent & confidence she had!*

*All the best for her future endeavours.*

## 'You instilled in me the values of integrity and balanced viewpoint'

Before I write anything else – let me confess to you that even though I joined the mass communications course in LU – I was not clear about my career – what profession I will be choosing or more precisely what will I be taking up as a profession. As you know, in those days, I used to teach but it was only after you provided support and guidance that it became clear to me about my passion towards writing and this profession.

I have had a lot of teachers in my life who have been quite helpful to me, but I think that we share a very special relationship that has no parallel. With you, I have always felt quite comfortable to share my personal challenges and always received valuable advice.

In any unconventional professional settings, I recall and implement your teachings, values and how you always mentioned the importance of keeping one's integrity and how keeping a balanced viewpoint is important while reporting and writing news stories.

I believe that I am only able to reach to this point because of a strong – thinking foundation that was given by you in my formative years. I will always be thankful to you for this.

As far as personal life is concerned, I always try and help my kid and my students – keeping in mind how you helped me and guided me. I take pride in trying to imitate you while helping my students.

Your values and teachings are right at the heart of what we do on a daily basis as part of our two media sites –

TelecomDrive.com and ChannelDrive.in. I am thankful to God and humbled with what we have achieved so far.

And today, if I look back, I don't see myself achieving anything close to what I have done today - if we have not met. Considering the fact that at one point in time (1997-98), I came very close to being selected for banking services (PO exams), thankfully I did not make it to the final round.

Thank you for always guiding me and having my back!

With love, Sir

Zia Askari

Founder & Editor TelecomDrive.com and ChannelDrive.in

***Comments***

*M.Sc. in Science Communication was a new PG program that Lucknow University introduced in late 90s, and Zia was one of the bright students from the day one.*

*He had a spark and was very focused to make his career in Science & Technology industry. I used to see his writing wherein he used to apply his technical knowledge in particular the IT sector.*

*Opportunities in the industry were not as open as we have these days. You only had to wait for a right opening.*

*PD Data Quest was an organization which was encouraging science writing. Though there was no regular opening, I asked Zia to prepare three different writings, and send it to the organization. Who knows it might click? And it worked with Zia taking his entry as Journalist (Technical Writer).*

*Its over 20 years now, and Zia is an Influencer enjoying a top position in Telecom sector. Zia believed Success to Mantra is to work hard with sincerity, discipline and consistency. Things will go your way one day.*

*At least he has proved it.*

**"A man who has always been a hustler at this stage of his life, and has mastered living life in a righteous way"**

It's been two years since I have graduated from college, and I still feel the bond I shared with you has only grown. From the very first week of college till now you have been my go-to person. There had been many instances in life where I had been perplexed in making the right decision for myself.

The mentor-mentee relation with you was never restricted to academia. There had been times you listened to my problems related to my family when I had issues in dealing with my friends and my love life. You used to always listen to me, understand my situation, and suggest me things that would take me in the right direction.

Sir, you always made a constant effort to push my boundaries and explore new areas related to my interests and hobbies and helped me nurture those skills during all this time.

It was during the start of the COVID -19 Pandemic, we all had freshly graduated at that time. Everyone was worried about their future. Hiring had stopped globally, people were losing jobs, and there were salary slashes. We all were worried about our job & career.

It was at that time I had got an idea to start a business during the pandemic. Doing a business at the start of my career was never a choice. The idea was weird, and I was quite unsure about whether it would be the right decision or not at the time of a global pandemic.

It was then I realized your words that we all are capable of doing what we think we can achieve even if the path seems unclear in the beginning. If we have made our mind, we'll make our way too.

This really helped me make the right decision for my career and you guided and supported me constantly through this as well.

I had the privilege to be guided by the best for all 5 years of my academic journey in college. You have been a constant pillar throughout this journey.

If I look back on my journey from a fresher in college to a working professional, there has been n number of instances where we had a difference in opinions. But you always encouraged me to speak my mind. Put out and question things.

I remember Sir, you used to tell me that I have a bossy attitude and this at times hinders my ability to be an effective and expressive communicator. It took me time to under that.

Now when I have to deal with different kinds of clients at work and at my office, I understand how you were right, and thanks to you that I worked upon myself and changed my attitude which now helps me in my professional and personal life.

In my personal life, I would say that I have tried imbibing your qualities as a person, the kind of attitude he has towards life, how you remain grounded with all that you have, how you have the ability to always be a learner; be it trying your hand at technology, acquiring new skills like as a photographer.

Thank you very much for being yourself and guiding me through-out.

With love, Sir,

Shagun Verma

Founder - Madhouse

Marketing Executive

Institute for Career Studies, Lucknow

***Comments***

*Shagun is credited for spending full five years with the institution first at Undergraduate and then continuing with her master's in Advertising & Marketing program. She has been the founder member of University Digital Club (UDC) at its launch. She didn't just lead it till the last day of her university but built a team of some 12 students' member.*

*She carried rich legacy of University's value and laid the strong foundation of the club which still carries on. In academics, she did very well, and earned the top honours. In true sense, she was 'Ms. Dependable.'*

*There was hardly an activity which was without Shagun! She did face some tough time with the family specially during the pandemic when she had to look for her placements and she took the risk of becoming an entrepreneur, and set up a venture Mad-House a media solution company and justified her decision to the course at PG.*

*Today she not only is well settled with her company but also working as a consultant to other organizations.*

*Well, done, Shagun, we all are proud of you.*

# Epilogue

It is with great responsibility and pleasure that I am writing my feelings, observations, and experience of 40 years about this very crucial relationship in the life of a student as well as a teacher. I have mentored many students and I can understand how Prof Johri must be feeling while compiling the experiences of his mentees, knowing their achievements and their present occupation. Prof. Johri has quoted some examples of mythological characters to emphasise this relationship, although each one of us has a mentor who has directly or indirectly, formally, or informally, mentored us on the path of rightness, success and growth in our career and helped us to achieving our goals.

The mentor-mentee relationship is **a** professional and an interpersonal relationship. It exists between a mentor and student/s also called a mentee. Mentors are different from coaches and act as guides to their mentees. They do this by offering advice and support, as well as helping them develop new skills.

The mentor-mentee relationship is one of the most crucial one, a student develops during his student life and career. Finding and working with a good mentor is a defining career moment for many students. One that accelerates professional growth and helps them meet both short-term and long-term goals. Once you gain significant experience, you can influence the next generation of students by becoming a mentor yourself.

The key to a successful mentor-mentee relationship is transparency on the part of both the mentor and mentee since if information is hidden by the mentee, the mentor will not be able to guide the mentee properly and vice versa if the mentor is hiding some crucial information, the mentee will not get proper advice. Feedback plays an essential role in mentorship. It's what allows the mentee to act and make decisions that help mentees achieve their goals. The mentor's feedback can help mentees avoid mistakes and save time in the process.

I appreciate Prof. Johri for being in touch with so many of his mentees and able to contact, coordinate with them and narrate their experience of being a mentee of Prof. Johri, I also appreciate all the mentees who responded to Prof. Johri timely and have shared their experiences. I do realize that the mentees in their careers are busy and sometimes find it difficult to respond to such requests.

One thing is very clear from the narrations of the students of Prof. Johri that he was a popular teacher amongst his students, and they had been counselled, guided, or advised by him during their student life and afterwards, the reason why so many of them responded.

I must appreciate the very idea of Prof. Johri to compile the experiences of his mentees in the form of a book and I am very sure that the readers will find this book a very interesting reading material and be motivated to search for a mentor if they still do not have one.

My very best wishes for a great success for this book.

**Prof. (Dr) Sunil Dhaneshwar**

**Pro Vice Chancellor**

**Amity University Uttar Pradesh**

**Lucknow campus**

Printed by Libri Plureos GmbH in Hamburg,
Germany